WASHINGTON

★ THE | GENERALS ★

WASHINGTON

A Legacy of Leadership

★ THE | GENERALS ★

Paul S. Vickery, Ph.D.

THOMAS NELSON
Since 1798

NASHVILLE   DALLAS   MEXICO CITY   RIO DE JANEIRO

Published in Nashville, Tennessee, by Thomas Nelson. Thomas Nelson is a registered trademark of Thomas Nelson, Inc.

Thomas Nelson, Inc., titles may be purchased in bulk for educational, business, fund-raising, or sales promotional use. For information, please e-mail SpecialMarkets@ThomasNelson. com.

Library of Congress Cataloging-in-Publication Data

Vickery, Paul S.
    George Washington : legacy of leadership / Paul S. Vickery.
        p. cm. -- (The generals)
    Includes bibliographical references and index.
    ISBN 978-1-59555-280-8 (alk. paper)
    1. Washington, George, 1732-1799--Military leadership. 2. Command of troops--Case studies. 3. Political leadership--United States--Case studies. 4. Generals--United States--Biography. 5. United States. Continental Army--Biography. 6. United States--History--Revolution, 1775-1783--Campaigns. 7. United States--Politics and government--1789-1797. I. Title.
    E312.25.V53 2011
    973.4'1092--dc22

                                2011003829

                    Printed in the United States of America

                    11 12 13 14 15 WOR 6 5 4 3 2 1

To Joyce, my wife, friend, and lover, whose love and support are responsible for any good thing I accomplish.

Contents

A Note from the Editor   ix

Prologue   xi

Introduction   xvii

    One: Preparation for Leadership   1

    Two: A Military Career Begins   11

    Three: Braddock's Defeat   23

    Four: Road to Revolution   37

    Five: Commander in Chief   49

    Six: New York   65

    Seven: Long Island   77

    Eight: Harlem Heights and White Plains   93

Nine: Trenton   105

Ten: Princeton   117

Eleven: Brandywine   131

Twelve: Germantown   141

Thirteen: Valley Forge   151

Fourteen: Monmouth   167

Fifteen: The Road to Yorktown   177

Sixteen: Victory   189

Seventeen: Presidency   209

Legacy   219

Notes   225

Bibliography   236

Acknowledgments   245

About the Author   247

A Note from the Editor

TO CONTEMPLATE THE lives of America's generals is to behold both the best of us as a nation and the lesser angels of human nature, to bask in genius and to be repulsed by arrogance and folly. It is these dichotomies that have defined the widely differing attitudes toward the "man on horseback," which have alternatively shaped the eras of our national memory. We have had our seasons of hagiography, in which our commanders can do no wrong and in which they are presented to the young, in particular, as unerring examples of nobility and manhood. We have had our revisionist seasons, in which all power corrupts—military power in particular—and in which the general is a reviled symbol of societal ills.

Fortunately, we have matured. We have left our adolescence

with its gushing extremes and have come to a more temperate view. Now, we are capable as a nation of celebrating Washington's gifts to us while admitting that he was not always a gifted tactician in the field. We can honor Patton's battlefield genius and decry the deformities of soul which diminished him. We can learn both from MacArthur at Inchon and from MacArthur at Wake Island.

We can also move beyond the mythologies of film and leaden textbook to know the vital humanity and the agonizing conflicts, to find a literary experience of war which puts the smell of boot leather and canvas in the nostrils and both the horror and the glory of battle in the heart. This will endear our nation's generals to us and help us learn the lessons they have to teach. Of this we are in desperate need, for they offer lessons of manhood in an age of androgyny, of courage in an age of terror, of prescience in an age of myopia, and of self-mastery in an age of sloth. To know their story and their meaning, then, is the goal here and in the hope that we will emerge from the experience a more learned, perhaps more gallant, and, certainly, more grateful people.

Stephen Mansfield
Series Editor, *The Generals*

Prologue

I consider it an indispensable duty to close this last solemn act
of my Official life, by commending the Interests of our dearest Country to the protection of Almighty God, and those who
have the superintendence of them, to his holy keeping.

—GEORGE WASHINGTON

ON DECEMBER 20, 1783, the city of Annapolis, Maryland,
was abuzz with the news that the most adored and admired
American was in town. The boom of thirteen cannons had
announced his arrival the previous day. "His Excellency" had
come to resign from the army that had, with the aid of the French,
defeated the most powerful military in the world and gained
independence for America. "Sir: I take the earliest opportunity
to inform Congress of my arrival in this City," Washington wrote

President of Congress Thomas Mifflin, "with the intention of asking leave to resign the Commission I have the honor of holding in their Service."[1]

The Treaty of Paris, signed just over three months previously, mandated that the British occupation army leave all American territory. Washington believed his duty was done. After saying a tearful good-bye to his officers in New York and Philadelphia, the gray-haired fifty-three-year-old General George Washington was to appear before the highest civilian authority in the land, the Confederation Congress, and tender his resignation.

The evening of the twenty-second he was feted by the Maryland elite. After thirteen toasts, accompanied by the boom of the same number of cannon, the ball began. Though Washington rarely smiled because of his bad teeth, he was a favorite with the ladies. "The General danced every set," wrote an observer, "that all the ladies might have the pleasure of dancing with him, or as it since has been handsomely expressed, get a touch of him."[2] Washington then left the party to put the finishing touches on his resignation speech.

Two days before Christmas, at precisely noon, he strode into the congressional chambers and addressed the representatives. Meanwhile, his belongings were being packed and his horse groomed and made ready for departure. Martha was waiting. He had promised to be at Mount Vernon for Christmas dinner. Mifflin and the nineteen or twenty other representatives—seated, with their hats on—greeted the general. Only seven states were represented, but a quorum had been declared for the purpose of receiving his letter.

As the-second floor gallery was opened, favored ladies rushed in to fill the seats. Both common citizens and elite vied for standing position along the wall. An expectant hush fell over the room as Mifflin stood, declared the meeting was in order, and addressed Washington. "Sir, the United States in Congress assembled," he boomed, "are prepared to receive your communications." The commander in chief formally rose to his full six-foot-two-inch height, bowed, and drew a letter from his breast pocket. The seated representatives doffed their hats but did not return the bow. With quivering hands, the old general read: "Mr. President: The great events on which my resignation depended having at length taken place; I have now the honor of offering my sincere Congratulations to Congress and of presenting myself before them to surrender into their hands the trust committed to me, and to claim the indulgence of retiring from the service of my country."[3]

Humbly, he played down his abilities during the war. "A diffidence in my abilities to accomplish so arduous a task," he continued, "which however was superseded by a confidence in the rectitude of our Cause, the support of the Supreme Power of the Union, and the patronage of Heaven." As he praised and gave credit to the officers who served with him, emotion gripped him. Pausing momentarily, undoubtedly reflecting on those long, cold, starving times at Valley Forge and Morristown, the scenes of bloody battle and defeat, the loss of so many good men, and the many battles with Congress, he forced himself to continue. Grasping his paper tightly, now with both hands, he continued. "It was impossible the choice of confidential officers to compose my family," he continued, struggling to steady the paper, "should have been more fortunate. Permit me, Sir, to recommend in particular those who have continued in Service to the present moment, as worthy of the favorable notice and patronage of Congress."[4] Many in the audience wiped their eyes as he concluded.

"I consider it an indispensable duty to close this last solemn act of my Official life, by commending the Interests of our dearest Country to the protection of Almighty God, and those who have the superintendence of them, to his holy keeping. Having now finished the work assigned me, I retire from the great theatre of action . . . I here offer my commission and take my leave of all the employments of public life."[5]

Washington then handed over his commission and a written copy of his statement, which lasted about three minutes, bowed again to the delegates—who doffed their hats once more—and left the room. After Congress formally adjourned, Washington returned, personally greeting each delegate. He then mounted his waiting horse and rode south. After spending a night on the road, he arrived at Mount Vernon and his beloved Martha just in time for dinner on Christmas Eve as he had promised.[6]

Thus began the interlude between the career of the military general—whose faith, valor, vision, and leadership had won the "Glorious Cause," as the revolution was known—and the political role of first president of the newly independent country. In a sense the former was the preparation for the latter: he learned to become the father of our country by first being the father of our military. That legacy of leadership, born in the face of adversity, would serve him well as he established many of the precedents that would be followed by those who succeeded him in the office of chief executive. Similarly, the discipline, order, and bravery of our armed forces directly reflect the legacy of Washington's example and leadership. It was as Henry Lee, a member of the Continental Congress from 1774 to 1780 and signer of the Declaration of the Independence, proclaimed at Washington's funeral in 1799:

> First in war—first in peace—and first in the hearts of his country-men, he was second to none in the humble and endearing scenes of private life; pious, just, humane, temperate, and sincere; uniform, dignified, and commanding, his example was as edifying to all around him as were the effects of that example lasting.[7]

The purpose of this volume is to examine the events that led to the transformation of George Washington from a twenty-one-year-old appointed major in the Virginia militia to the commander in chief of the American forces. Experiences gained during his younger days laid the groundwork—by developing the character and training the mind, even as it toughened his body—for future greatness. The crucible of his early frontier experiences—his successes and his failures—forged the tactics and strategies that allowed his poorly fed, raggedly equipped, multicultural rabble of untrained soldiers to succeed on the battlefield. In so doing, Washington established what became the armed forces of the United States and created a legacy for all future American leaders to follow.

A word about faith: Although this work is not primarily intended to emphasize the religious faith of Washington, his dependence upon and belief in the power of God is evident in his writings. The specifics of his faith, though, have long been debated, his supposed Deism held in tension with his obvious Anglican beliefs. Here, we shall allow his words to speak for themselves. In this way it will be possible to understand fully how George Washington believed himself to be, as he often said, "in the hands of a good Providence."[8]

Introduction

I not being so good a Woodsman as the rest of my Company
striped myself very orderly & went in to the Bed as they call'd
it when to my Surprize I found it to be nothing but a Little
Straw . . . one Thread Bare blanket with double its Weight of
Vermin such as Lice Fleas &c.

—GEORGE WASHINGTON

IN EIGHTEENTH-CENTURY AMERICA there were
two ways of becoming wealthy. One was through shipping and
trade with Europe and the Caribbean. The other was agricultural
development, the route to riches employed by many in the southern colonies.

Other than Charleston, South Carolina (a major shipping
port and the fourth largest city in America in 1730 with nearly

11,000 residents, then known as Charles Town), the mostly rural South, where 80 percent of the population was agriculturally employed, fostered a somewhat rigid class system. Wealthy planters, or "gentlemen," were at the top, poor white farmers were second-class citizens, and slaves were at the bottom. In the much more formal South, character or how one conducted one's affairs, was highly esteemed. In the larger, much less personal and more egalitarian northern cities—such as Philadelphia, with a 1730 population of 11,500, New York, with nearly 12,000 residents; and Boston with a population of 13,000—the social structure was much more fluid. These centers of trade were surrounded by small family farms.

Yet with its abundant land and rich tobacco crops, Virginia relied on large plantations. Land and slaves were the basis of its wealth—and into this world George Washington was born.

We really know relatively little about Washington's early life. Stories of his cutting down the cherry tree and his inability to lie about it, first written about by Parson Mason Locke Weems in 1800, were probably intended to demonstrate Washington's character rather than to relate factual incidents.[1] Certainly honesty was one of Washington's most esteemed virtues. He was never accused of lying and seems to have been a boy and a man contented with simple things. It was throughout his life as he described nearly ten years before his death to Reverend William Gordon, "For the great Searcher of human hearts knows there is no wish in mine, beyond that of living and dying an honest man, on my own farm."[2]

Washington was born into a family of moderate wealth on February 11, 1732 (during his life a change in the calendar converted this to February 22, 1732), in Westmoreland County, Virginia. When he was six, his parents, Augustine and Mary Ball Washington, moved to Ferry Farm, located across the Rappahannock River from Fredericksburg, Virginia. Augustine had been previously married to Jane Butler, by whom he had three children: Lawrence, Augustine Jr., and Jane. After the death of his first wife, Augustine married Mary Ball and together they had five children: George, Betty, Samuel, John Augustine, and Charles. On April 12, 1743, Augustine Washington died suddenly, leaving Ferry Farm to eleven-year-old George. The boy became very attached to his older half-brother, Lawrence, who stepped into the role of surrogate father.

Although details about his early education are sketchy, it seems young George was tutored by an Anglican layman. Throughout his life, Washington conceded his limited education, but constantly sought to improve himself by reading and studying. David Humphreys, a friend and early biographer, wrote that he "was betimes instructed in the principles of grammar, the theory of reasoning, on speaking, the science of numbers, the elements of geometry, and the highest branches of mathematics, the art of mensuration [measuring], composing together with the rudiments of geography, history and the studies which are not improperly called 'the humanities.'"[3]

In addition, the physically imposing Washington received training in the social graces such as fencing, dancing, and riding—all of which were highly prized in southern society and in all of which he excelled. Because he was especially accomplished at dancing and polite conversation, he was often invited to the social activities of his wealthy and politically successful neighbors. Washington also became a skilled horseman and was celebrated for his strength. Humphreys recounted that Washington claimed "he never met any man who could throw a stone to so great a distance as himself."[4] Very early in life, Washington recognized the value of appearances and worked hard at creating and maintaining both his reputation and demeanor.

Recognizing the responsibilities of a Virginia gentleman, the young man set out to learn how to become one. Before his sixteenth birthday, after careful research and thought, Washington wrote out a list of 110 "Rules of Civility and Decent Behaviour in Company and Conversation." Drawn from many sources, number 2 dealt with such social restrictions as "When in company put not your Hand to any Part of the Body not usually Discovered." Number 23 advised on social justice: "When you see a Crime punished, you may be inwardly Pleased; but always shew Pity to the Suffering Offender." The future general probably reflected long on number 67: "Detract not from others neither be excessive in Commanding." Finally, number 110 dealt with character formation: "Labor to keep alive in your Breast that Little Spark of Celestial fire called Conscience."[5]

Washington received his moral and spiritual training both from the Anglican Church and his mother. "Mrs. Washington was connected with the church there [St. George's Anglican Church], and her son no doubt shared, under her own eye, the benefits of divine worship, and such religion instruction as mothers in that day were eminently accustomed to give their children," writes one biographer. "It was the habit to teach the young the first principles of religion according to the formularies of the church." These "formularies" consisted of "the fear of God, and strict adherence of the moral virtues, such as truth, justice, charity, humility, modesty, temperance, chastity, and industry."[6] As we shall observe, Washington attempted to maintain these moral and spiritual virtues throughout his life. In the midst of his academic, physical, and moral training, his practical knowledge of both nature and humanity also increased.

A lover of the rugged outdoors, Washington often roamed the family estate along the Potomac. After his father's death, he moved to Lawrence's home at Mount Vernon, a much larger estate. Lawrence had married into the wealthy Fairfax family. After George's mother put her foot down and refused his request to go to sea in 1748 (at age sixteen), Lawrence's father-in-law, William Fairfax, hired George to survey his vast holdings in the Shenandoah Valley.

In "A Journal of My Journey Over the Mountains," recorded during this first adventure, we get a first glimpse into the activities and ideas of the future first president of the United States. He naturally took to the outdoor life, commenting on the scenery and recounting his hunting adventures. "This Morning Shot twice at wild Turkies but killd none," he recorded on April 1, 1748. On Sunday the third, he wrote that a storm had struck: "We had our Tent Carried Quite off with the Wind and was obliged to Lie the Latter part of the Night without covering." He seemed more pleased with this arrangement than when he spent the night in an inn. There he found his bed to be "nothing but a Little Straw— Matted together without Sheets . . . but only one Thread Bear blanket with double its Weight of Vermin such as Lice Fleas &c.

[etc.].″ After this experience he promised "not to Sleep so from that time forward chusing rather to sleep in the open Air before a fire . . .″[7]

Apparently George did well on his first surveying position, because after his return he was appointed surveyor in Culpeper County, Virginia—an impressive feat for a seventeen-year-old. Between assignments there and in the Shenandoah Valley, Washington also surveyed his own Ferry Farm or Lawrence's Mount Vernon. Soon, though, life was to become more difficult for the young gentleman.

While Washington was employed as a surveyor, Lawrence became ill. Failing to find a cure in England, he sought the healthier climate of the Caribbean. Together the brothers traveled to Barbados in September 1751. George enjoyed the novelties of both the social activities and discovering new tropical fruits, such as the "avagado pair" [avocado] and "Pine Apple."[8] Lawrence's health failed to improve, though, and even George came down with a mild case of smallpox. Although annoying at the time, this minor setback may have saved his life; in the future many would suffer and die of smallpox while Washington remained immune.

Realizing he was dying, Lawrence decided to return to his beloved Mount Vernon. He spent his last days arranging his affairs and in July 1752 passed from this life. With his death, the twenty-year-old George took over the management of Mount Vernon (and ownership some years later), making him a significant landholder; Washington also took over his brother's post with the Virginia militia, launching of his storied military career.

ONE

Preparation for Leadership

I can't say that ever in my Life I suffer'd so much Anxiety as I did in this affair.

—GEORGE WASHINGTON

There are no secrets to success. It is the result of preparation, hard work, and learning from failure.

—GEN. COLIN POWELL

IF EVER A life fit the description of "preparation, hard work, and learning from failure," it was that of George Washington. Viewed in hindsight, his entire life was a preparation for the role he would play in the American Revolution and as the nation's first president. His early years display the faith, ambition, work ethic, and character of the man that he became.

1

At the age of twenty-one, in February 1753, Washington began his military career when he was appointed major in the Southern District of Virginia by Governor Robert Dinwiddie. As adjutant of the militia his duties were not taxing and he was able to continue to develop his skills as a surveyor. Personally, he owned about two thousand acres of land; after Lawrence's death the potential existed to inherit even more.

Thus he began the life of a Virginia landowner, part-time officer, and aspiring gentleman. In 1758, his friend George Mercer described Washington as "straight as an Indian, 6 foot 2 inches in his stockings and weighing 175 pounds." He was "a splendid horseman," and his "movements and gestures are graceful, his walk majestic."[1] Although he focused his attentions on improving the gentlemanly pursuits of riding, land acquisition, and planting, world events would change the course of his life.

During the late seventeenth and early eighteenth centuries, both the French and English had discovered that wealth was to be made by trading with the Indians in the Ohio River Valley. Formed where the Allegheny and Monongahela Rivers merge to become the Ohio and site of present-day Pittsburgh, the area was known at that time as "the Forks." Both nations recognized that control of the Forks was the key to possession of the entire valley. Both nations desired the profits of the rich fur trade and abundant raw materials available there. Both also believed they had a legal claim to the area—the French because of the travels of LaSalle in 1669–70, and the British as a westward extension of Virginia and Pennsylvania. The British also insisted the 1744 Treaty of Lancaster made with the Iroquois gave them legal ownership.

But in 1748 the Iroquois gave assurances to the French that they had not ceded the territory. Native Americans did not believe in individual ownership of land. Although they might claim tribal control of an area, land—indeed all nature—was the possession only of heaven. Therefore no chief or individual tribe had the authority to cede lands, they believed.

Governor Dinwiddie, who was also a partner in one of the first land speculation companies in America, the Ohio Company, was concerned. French occupation of the Forks threatened his interests. "I hope you will think it necessary to prevent the French taking Possession of the Lands on the Ohio . . ." Dinwiddie wrote the Board of Trade; "indeed in my private Opinion they ought to be prevented making any Settlements to the Westward of Our present Possessions." In August of 1753, the Crown responded by giving Dinwiddie the authority to discover the location of the French. If settled in the disputed area, he was to ask them to leave. If they refused, he had the authority "to drive them off by Force of Arms." With royal approval granted, Dinwiddie prepared to send an expedition to locate the trespassers and present them with a letter ordering them to leave.[2]

Major Washington, adjutant general for the southern district of Virginia, eagerly volunteered and was selected to lead this delegation. His mission was to find the French commander, present his credentials and Dinwiddie's letter, and demand an explanation for their presence. The directions also specified that he should seek intelligence concerning the number and placement of the French forces. Upon hiring the Dutchman Jacob Vanbraam as interpreter and Christopher Gist as guide, along with four others, Washington set out, eager to fulfill his mission. True to form, he departed on the same day he received his commission—October 31, 1753.

As was his habit, Washington maintained a journal of his experiences. In it he confirmed what his responsibilities were and how he was to conduct them. He recognized that he was a man under authority and understood he was to follow the orders of his superiors and carry these out to the best of his abilities. Obedience to orders was a lesson he had learned early and this principle became fundamental to his nature. After trudging over eighty miles in three weeks during "excessive Rains & vast Quantity of Snow," his party arrived at a small trading post established by a Mr. Fraser at the mouth of Turtle Creek, about ten miles north of present day Pittsburgh.[3]

Perhaps because of his training as a surveyor, Washington had a keen eye for the terrain. "I spent some Time in viewing the Rivers, & the Land in the Fork," he wrote in his journal, "which I think extreamly well situated for a Fort as it has absolute Command of both Rivers." He described the depth, width, and speed of the rivers. This was critical. In the eighteenth century, waterways were the key to transportation. Since "roads" were little more than improved animal paths, rivers were highways of trade and movement.[4]

The French needed control of the Ohio River, as it connected their settlements in Canada with those in the Illinois Territory and eventually to their colony in New Orleans. The British viewed control of the rivers as essential to the opening up, development, and settlement of the western lands. Thus the stakes were high as to who held control over the Ohio River Valley.

Washington then went to make contact with the natives. Traveling thirteen miles over "some extream good & bad Land" his party arrived at the village of Logstown, where Washington encountered four French deserters from New Orleans. "I enquir'd into the Situation of the French on the Mississippi," he chronicled, "their Number & what Forts they had Built." It was also at Logstown where he met Tanacharison (also known as "Half King"), a chief who claimed to speak for the Iroquois Confederacy. Washington had wisely brought twists of tobacco and other presents for the Indians and immediately gained their goodwill.[5]

Washington inquired about the French presence in the area. Tanacharison had just returned from a confrontation with the French at the nearest fort, French Creek, which was not "under 5 or 6 Nights Sleep, good Traveling." There he met the arrogant French commander, who had insulted him. "I am not affraid of Flies or Musquito's;" the Frenchman had scoffed, "for Indians are such as those." Should the English or anyone else try to block the river, he possessed sufficient strength "to burst it open, & tread under my Feet" any opposition. Several days later Washington and his party, led by Half King and three Indians, left for the trading post at Venango.[6]

Constant rain, snow, and drizzle complicated the nearly seventy-mile trek. On December 4, they met the fort commander, Captain Phillipe Thomas de Joncaire. "He invited us to Sup with them," wrote Washington, "and treated with the greatest Complaisance." Soon the French tongues were loosened. "The Wine, as they dos'd themselves pretty plentifully . . . gave license to their Tongues to reveal their Sentiments more freely." Keeping a cool head and wisely restraining himself from imbibing, Washington listened and observed. Though he hid his feelings, Washington was astounded that they provided him with the number of troops and location of their forts. The French recognized the British had a two-to-one numerical superiority, but boasted they "were too slow & dilatory to prevent any Undertaking of theirs." After dinner, Washington presented Dinwiddie's letter. Joncaire refused to accept it, explaining he did not have the authority to do so. They would have to go to Fort Le Boeuf, roughly sixty miles away.[7]

Although he had privately gloated over the intelligence he had learned, Washington was shocked to realize he'd underestimated the cunning of Joncaire, who plied the Indians with liquor and gifts and urged them to remain with the French. Only after Gist confronted Half King "with great Perswasion" did he agree to leave. Departing on December 7, the journey was slowed "by excessive rains, Snows, & bad traveling, through many Mires & Swamps." Finally, on December 11, the frozen, wet party arrived at Fort Le Boeuf.[8]

There they met Jacques Le Gardeur de Saint-Pierre, a knight of the Royal and Military Order of St. Louis. Washington described him as "an elderly Gentleman, & has much the Air of a Soldier." Washington presented Dinwiddie's letter to him and awaited a response. The French officers withdrew to consider the matter, leaving Washington with the run of the fort. He used his time wisely, subtly making sketches of the fort, fixing the disposition and number of weapons, and the size and location of buildings. "I cou'd get no certain Account of the Number of Men here," he reported, "but according to the best Judgement I cou'd form, there is an Hundred exclusive of Officers, which are pretty many." He also ordered a count of the number of canoes available to transport forces south in the spring, "50 of Birch Bark, & 170 of Pine; besides many others that were block'd out, in Readiness to make." He was now anxious to get back to Williamsburg and report his findings.[9]

On the evening of the fourteenth, Washington received the reply he had been waiting for and attempted to leave on the fifteenth. The French, however, had again plied the Indian guides with alcohol; guns and other presents would follow if Tanacharison refused to accompany Washington. Half King made it abundantly clear he wanted to remain with the French and Washington became worried. "I can't say that ever in my Life I suffer'd so much Anxiety as I did in this affair," he noted. The French used "every Stratagem that the most fruitful Brain cou'd invent" to get the Indians to remain. Finally, an angered and frustrated Washington put his foot down and "press'd him in the strongest Terms to go." On the sixteenth, Half King relented and together they began the journey home.[10]

The six-day trip back to Venango was made by canoe down a narrow, crooked river filled with rocks and ice. Snow pelted them and several times they had to get into the freezing water for as much as thirty minutes to get over shoals. At one point the ice became so hard they needed to portage the canoe a quarter mile, where they joined the horses that had been sent on ahead.

After resting a day in Venango, Washington was ready to leave on the twenty-third. Half King, pleading illness, asked to wait a few days. Frustrated and anxious to get the French letter back to Dinwiddie, Washington left the next day, according to Gist, "in Indian dress." As the weather got colder and the roads filled with snow that froze at night, the horses sickened, forcing Washington to continue on foot. Three days later, in order to make better time, he decided to leave the horses and baggage with Vanbraam and continue with Gist.[11]

The next day after passing a place called Murdering Town, they met a party of French Indians who apparently were waiting for them. In his own diary, Gist provided a much more complete account of what happened next. One of the Indians called Gist by name and Gist seemed to recognize him and asked him to act as guide. They moved "very brisk for eight or ten miles," recorded Gist. Washington was now weary and his feet hurt, so he wanted to make camp. The guide urged them on as his camp was only "two whoops" away. As they came into an open field, separated by fifteen feet, "The Indian made a stop, turned about; the Major [Washington] saw him point his gun toward us and fire." Before he could reload, they wrestled his gun away. Gist wanted to kill him but Washington passed it off as an accident. At about nine o'clock they let him go, giving him a piece of bread, and then hustled away, traveling all night to prevent his joining up with others and following them.[12]

After traveling through the night and most of the next day, they arrived at the Allegheny River. They expected to cross on frozen ice. The river, however, was not frozen but full of chunks of floating ice. Using "one poor Hatchet," they cut trees and tied together a makeshift raft "after a whole days Work." In the freezing weather they set off across the river using poles as oars. About halfway across, the raft became jammed by the ice and "we expected every Moment our Raft wou'd sink, & we Perish." To get free, Washington stuck his pole in the river. The current was so violent that "it Jirk'd me into 10 Feet Water." Desperately he grabbed a log and struggled to hold on until Gist pulled him out. They were forced to spend a miserably cold, wet night on a small island. "The Cold was so extream severe," recorded Washington, that Mr. Gist got all his Fingers & some of his Toes Froze." The good news was that night the river froze solid so they could walk across the next morning.[13]

Two days later, on January 1, 1754, Washington arrived at Fraser's trading post, bought a horse, and left alone for Williamsburg. Arriving on the sixteenth, he "waited upon His Honour the Governor with the Letter I had brought from the French Commandant and to give an Account of the Procedures of my Journey." He was anxious to report "the most remarkable Occurrences that happen'd to me."[14]

The twenty-one-year-old had successfully completed his first military mission. Demonstrating courage and persistence and making on-the-spot decisions, he had learned valuable lessons in leadership. His self-confidence rose dramatically as he had commanded men and survived two life-threatening experiences. Washington's first military expedition as ambassador to the French was considered such a success that the governor later published *The Journal of Major George Washington*. Washington's next mission, however, would allow him to hear the sound of bullets and smell the smoke of battle.

TWO

A Military Career Begins

I heard bullets whistle . . . there was something charming in the sound.

—GEORGE WASHINGTON

THE YOUNG MAJOR couldn't have known that the news in the letter he carried back to the governor would begin a chain of events culminating in a war that would be fought not only on the American continent but around the world. Dinwiddie's letter had ordered the French to leave the Ohio Valley; the French response was not what he wanted to hear. "As to the summons you send me to retire," wrote Le Gardeur de Saint-Pierre, "I do not think myself obliged to obey it." The French were not budging. In fact, they determined to expand their fort building in the area.[1]

Dinwiddie immediately made Washington's journal public,

11

describing both his adventures and the French response. Published in colonial newspapers and in London, the *Journal of Major George Washington* both popularized the western frontier and provided Washington certain fame. He was even voted a bonus of fifty pounds sterling from the Virginia House of Burgess.[2]

The Crown commissioned Dinwiddie; if the French remained in the Ohio Valley he was "to drive them out by force of arms."[3] Seeking to fulfill this royal mandate (and, of course, to protect his financial interests in the Ohio Company), he appealed for troops from the other colonies, though the request fell upon deaf ears. Even the young major could raise no militia. If patriotism could not inspire volunteers, though, perhaps money could. After much discussion, the Virginia House of Burgesses allotted Dinwiddie 10,000 pounds sterling to prosecute the action. Washington wanted to play a role and quickly made his intentions known.

"The command of the whole forces is what I neither look for, expect, nor desire," he wrote in a letter to House member Richard Corbin. He would be content to be second in command and receive "the post of lieutenant-colonel." Should Corbin recommend him, however, he would, of course, "entertain a true sense of the kindness." Washington received his commission and a professor of mathematics, Joshua Fry, was appointed commander.[4]

With the promise of pay, enlistments began. Unfortunately the quality of the men was not what Washington was used to. "We daily Experience the great necessity for Cloathing the Men," he complained to Dinwiddie, "as we find the generallity of those who are to be Enlisted, are of those loose, Idle Persons that are quite destitute of House, and Home." Making matters worse, the promised pay was slow in coming.[5]

On April 2, 1754, with less than two hundred poorly trained and equipped men, Washington departed from Williamsburg. His orders were to proceed to the Forks and assist in the building of a fort supposedly already begun by a detachment of the Ohio Company. "You are to act on the defensive," read his orders. Should anyone hamper the efforts, however, "you are to . . . make prisoners of or to kill & destroy them."[6]

While en route, Washington received startling news. Captain Claude Pierre Pecaudy de Contrecouer and nearly 1,000 French soldiers had ejected Ensign Edward Ward, his men, and Half King from the Forks, and destroyed their fledgling fort. Worse, the French were building their own fort on the site. As Colonel Fry had not yet arrived, Washington had a decision to make. In a move that he was to follow throughout his military career, he called a council of war. To maintain the support of the Indians, Washington wrote a letter to Half King. He assured him that his current small force was only an advance guard and was "Clearing the Roads for a great Number of our Warriours that are immediately to follow with our Great Guns, our Ammunition, and our Provisions."[7]

Meanwhile, the French were busy building at the Forks. Fort Duquesne would have twelve-foot-thick log and earth walls, a dry moat, contain eight cannon, and be large enough to house two hundred men—a substantial nut for the British to crack.[8] Aware of the Virginian presence in the area, Contrecouer sent Ensign Joseph Coulon de Jumonville to intercept and order the British off of the disputed territory.

On May 24, Washington and his band of 160 arrived at Great Meadows, some fifty miles south of his destination, where he established camp, grateful for the plentiful water and forage. His men were exhausted by the construction of a road through the wilderness, which he hoped would soon carry Fry, his reinforcements, and cannon. Hacking, sawing, and digging, they had made only two to three miles a day progress.

Soon a messenger arrived with a letter from Half King, transcribed by a semiliterate John Davidson: "An acct of a french armey to meat Miger Georg Wassiontton therfor my Brotheres I deisir you to be awar of them for deisind to strike the forist Englsh they see tow deays since they marchd I cannot tell what nomber the hilf King and the rest of the Chiefes will be with you in five dayes to Consel."[9]

Fearing an attack, Washington ordered his men to dig in and remain alert. In a letter to Dinwiddie, he explained they had "made a good Intrenchment and by clearing the Bushes out of these Meadows prepar'd a charming field for an Encounter." On the twenty-seventh, his friend Gist arrived at camp and advised Washington that about fifty French soldiers were recently at his house, just thirteen miles away. Later that evening a message from Half King informed Washington that the French were vulnerable and located at "a low obscure place."[10]

What happened next is best told in Washington's own words. He and Tanacharison agreed to scout out the French position and "fall on them together." After sending out scouts to get the lay of the land, Washington wrote,

> We formed ourselves for an engagement, marching one after the other, in the Indian manner: We were advanced pretty near to them as we thought, when they discovered us; whereupon I ordered my company to fire . . . the greater part of the action, which only lasted a quarter of an hour, before the enemy was routed.
>
> We killed Mr. de Jumonville, the commander of that party, as also nine others . . . The Indians scalped the dead, and took away the most part of their arms.[11]

It was a mixed victory. In his first battle, Washington was unable to restrain the Indians he commanded. He also attacked what was essentially a diplomatic mission. His actions precipitated what was called the French and Indian War in America and the Seven Years' War in Europe. Clearly his orders gave him the authority, but did he have the judgment necessary to make such a decision? He obviously believed he had done the right thing.

In a letter to his brother John, Washington bragged he had been in the thick of the battle, exposed to enemy fire, and escaped unwounded. "I can with truth assure you, I heard Bulletts whistle," he boasted, "and believe me there was something charming in the sound." Perhaps it was youthful exuberance or perhaps he was merely relieved to have survived his first battle, but Washington would soon tire of the sound of battle and agree with King George III. After hearing of Washington's words, the king is reputed to have said, "He would not say so, if he had been used to hear very many."[12]

The day after the battle, May 29, Washington wrote Dinwiddie providing a brief account of the action. He accused the French of being spies. "Their intentions were evil," he quoted Half King, and they had "bad hearts." Fearing a retaliatory attack, he ordered the completion of a palisade. On June 2, after completing the aptly named Fort Necessity, Washington reported, "We had prayers in the fort." He would need divine help, as both white and Indian families soon arrived seeking protection. The French were sure to counterassault.[13]

The fort—seven feet high and about fifty feet in diameter, made of split logs—held some sixty to seventy men. The rest of his forces would have to rely upon trenches dug around its exterior. Because Washington was inexperienced and expected a frontal assault, he had the fort built a mere sixty yards from enfilading fire from the sloping forest. He certainly had confidence in his creation, recording that he did not fear "the attack of 500 Men." Tanacharison was less sanguine, calling it "that little thing upon the meadow."[14]

During the month of June, Washington received reinforcements. Two hundred Virginians arrived, bringing with them nine swivel guns, capable of firing two-pound balls, and much needed supplies. Also arriving a few days after this was an independent company of British regulars from South Carolina, commanded by Captain James Mackay. Whose arrival led to difficulties. Because he held a royal commission, Mackay refused to recognize the appointed Lieutenant Colonel Washington's authority.

Washington was unconcerned, though. He knew that Colonel James Innes, the commander since Fry had been killed in an accident, and four hundred North Carolina volunteers plus two companies of regular troops, were also on the way. The command structure would right itself shortly.

Expecting reinforcements, Washington continued clearing and building a road through the wilderness. It was hot, hard, backbreaking work and progress was excruciatingly slow. Horses died, wagons broke, and the men themselves became beasts of burden. Eventually they made it to Gist's camp and met with delegations from the Delaware, Shawnee, and Mingo tribes, as well as Tanacharison. As intelligent and experienced warriors, the natives could tell which way the wind was blowing. Washington had a ragtag army of about four hundred, with few supplies and only a hope that more were on the way. The French had a strong fort at Fort Duquesne at the Forks with over one thousand well-supplied troops. Why should they risk their lives and that of their families to fight with the British?[15]

After hearing of a strong French force moving against him, Washington decided he would return the twelve miles to Fort Necessity and make a stand. Traveling three days, with only handfuls of parched corn to eat, he and his men arrived on July 1. Discouraged that no help had come, Washington contemplated further retreat, but he knew his men had nothing left. They were spent. Perhaps rumors of independent troops coming from New York were true. Deciding to make his stand, he pushed his men to fortify their "little thing upon the meadow." Indian allies, including Half King, sensing disaster, slipped away into the wilderness.

Before he died, Tanacharison described Washington as "a good natured man, but had no Experience." Washington was a leader, however, and demonstrated bravery by "always driving them on to fight by his own Directions."[16]

Upon arrival at Fort Necessity, Washington's scouts reported the French were nearby at Redstone. Led by Louis Coulon de Villiers, the brother of the slain de Jumonville, the French approached along the road so painstakingly constructed by Washington. Wanting to visit his brother's grave, de Villiers stopped at the glen. Finding only scalped remnants of bodies, he ordered their burial. Furious at the murder of his brother and bent on revenge, de Villiers continued his pursuit of the assassins, arriving July 3.

At midday, de Villiers, with a combined French and Indian force of one thousand, surprised the exhausted and starving Virginians. Mackay's regulars held firm and fired a volley, while the scared militia quickly retreated inside the fort. In a driving rain the French occupied the wooded slopes just sixty yards away. Easily able to pick off anything that moved, they killed horses, cattle, even the dogs. The colonials hid in their soaking trenches, unable even to keep their powder dry. "We continued this unequal Fight, with an Enemy sheltered behind the Trees, ourselves without Shelter, in Trenches full of Water, in a settled Rain," reported Washington later, "and the Enemy galling us on all Sides incessantly from the Woods."[17] At eight o'clock that evening, Washington heard the words "*Voulez vous parler?*" Do you want to parley? Although Washington's men were only too happy to respond, he sensed a ruse.

Why did Coullon de Villiers want to talk? He had all the advantages. The colonials were not going anywhere and they could either be picked off or starved out. Perhaps de Villiers believed the rumors that English reinforcements were near or he realized the two nations were not technically at war. Perhaps the French were running low on supplies. In any case, Washington suspected deceit.[18]

Initially, Washington refused to parley. After assessing his situation, though—and undoubtedly hearing the groans of the wounded and recognizing that about a third of his able-bodied troops were either dead or wounded, he had at best three days of food available, his weapons and powder were soaked, some of his men had found the rum supply and over imbibed, and having no assurance of coming aid—he reconsidered. Suspecting a trap and not wanting the French to see the weakness of his situation, Washington sent out Van Braam and another French-speaking volunteer.

Van Braam negotiated the final agreement with the French. He returned in the pouring rain, holding the soggy capitulation de Villiers had handwritten on a scrap of paper. The ink ran as Van Braam struggled to translate the French and 250-plus years later it is impossible to know how he verbally translated the word *l'assasinat*. Washington understood it as "loss," "death," or "killing," and later claimed he was "deceived by our interpreter in regard to the word assassination" (by mistake or on purpose). Nonetheless, in effect Washington admitted to assassinating de Jumonville. He later was adamant that had he known how this would be interpreted, he never would have capitulated. The French believed he admitted to murdering de Jumonville, and this was the story publicized.[19]

Washington also agreed to leave the swivel guns at Fort Necessity, to vacate the Ohio Valley, and to leave two officers as prisoners. These would be returned when the French prisoners he had taken earlier were released. The date of his surrender was July 4, 1754. Certainly this date would always hold special significance for him.

Washington and his men left Fort Necessity, relieved at not being left to the mercy of the Indians, with their honor intact and their colors flying. They left thirty dead and carried seventy wounded, many severely. After burning what remained of the fort, the French left for Fort Duquesne, believing they had a confession of guilt for the death of de Jumonville and had expelled the British from the Forks.

By the time Washington arrived in Wills Creek, about fifty miles away, his army was in tatters. The men had received no pay and there were daily desertions. Finally, on July 17, 1754, he arrived at Williamsburg where he was generally regarded as a hero. Blame was placed on the colonies that had failed to send the promised troops. In a letter dated September 15, John Robinson wrote that the House of Burgesses "have taken particular Notice of the Bravery of Yourself, and the rest of the Officers and Soldiers under your command in the gallant Defense of your Country and have ordered me to return you their Thanks for it . . ."[20]

Washington had little opportunity to bask in praise. Within two months Governor Dinwiddie disbanded the Virginia Regiment. In its place he formed independent companies of one hundred men, each commanded by a captain, eliminating

Washington's position as colonel. Washington resigned in anger. "I must be reduced to a very low Command, and subjected to that of many who have acted as my inferior Officers," he explained to Colonel William Fitzhugh. "In short, every Captain, bearing the King's Commission; every half-pay Officer, or other, appearing with such commission, would rank before me." He would retire, with the sure knowledge that he had "opened the way when the smallness of our numbers exposed us to the attacks of a Superior Enemy. That I have hitherto stood the heat and brunt of the Day, and escaped untouched, in time of extreme danger; and that I have the Thanks of my Country for the Services I have rendered it." His self-righteous breast-beating ended with, "My inclinations are strongly bent to arms."[21]

How, then, do we assess the preliminary actions of the future general? He fired on a French force when their respective nations were at peace, but acted under orders. He allowed Indians under his command to murder and scalp wounded and helpless prisoners; yet how could he have controlled those whose culture dictated they take a visible symbol of their victory? He selected a particularly bad spot to build his fort and exaggerated its ability for defense, but he believed that troops and supplies were rushing to his aid. (Also, his men were too weary to continue the retreat.) Being defeated by a superior military force was no shame. Obviously he wrote his diaries and letters showing himself in the most favorable light and downplayed mistakes. He was ambitious, yet appeared humble. He was aggressive, yet appeared the victim. His life would be full of seeming contradictions.

One fact stands out among all the rest: his actions started

a war. Historian Alan Axelrod best describes the result of what came to be called the Great Meadows battle:

> Here began the French and Indian War, the commencement and North American theater of the cataclysmic Seven Years' War, truly the first "world" war, engulfing Europe, India, the Caribbean, and vast portions of the Atlantic Ocean, killing some 900,000 combatants, and savagely recarving the political contours of the planet.[22]

The lessons learned from these early defeats would later serve Washington and his country well. He had demonstrated courage, determination, and physical strength—and he would need them later as he became the model for those serving under him. He also learned the value of good intelligence, the necessity of having adequate supplies, and the importance of choosing the right place for battle. These lessons would come back to him in battles yet to come.[23]

THREE

Braddock's Defeat

[Washington was] a particular favorite of heaven, who could
never die in battle.

—ELDERLY CHIEF

AFTER RESIGNING HIS commission in the Virginia militia, Washington leased Mount Vernon from Lawrence's widow, Ann Fairfax. She had inherited the property upon the death of their young daughter, Sarah, in 1754. In addition to the land, he also received the service of the slaves assigned to that land. His rent, to be paid every Christmas Day, was "Fifteen thousand pounds of Tobacco in fifteen Hogsheads to be delivered out at one or some of the Warehouses in the County of Fairfax . . ." Washington could also pay in cash at the going rate. His first rent was due Christmas 1755. Events, however, had been set in motion that would interrupt his planter's life.[1]

King George II was unhappy about the French presence in what he considered British territory. He, therefore, sent fifty-nine-year-old Major General Edward Braddock, a career soldier who had never seen combat but was considered "a good disciplinarian and a skilled administrator, and . . . esteemed as a brave and honest officer" to Virginia. Braddock brought two regiments of British regulars with him. These were the Forty-Fourth and Forty-Eighth regiments of foot brought from garrison duty in Ireland. They arrived February 20, 1755. Also accompanying Braddock was his principal aide-de-camp Captain Robert Orme.[2]

On March 2, 1755, Orme invited Washington to become a part of Braddock's military "family." Orme knew that Washington was familiar with the terrain in the Ohio Valley and he also knew about the proud man's resignation over the issue of rank. Orme assured him that Braddock would handle any "disagreeableness" about Washington's rank. As one of the general's aides, he would be outside the normal chain of command and take orders only from Braddock. Hoping to impress Braddock and gain his patronage to receive a royal commission, Washington readily accepted. In a most ingratiating manner, he professed his great desire to "serve (with my best abilitys) my King & Country," and also affirmed that his goal was "to attain a small degree of knowledge in the military art."[3]

On April 21, 1755, a frustrated Braddock joined his army in Frederick Town, Maryland. Instead of the bustling activity of training and supplies pouring in, he found idle men and few supplies. He was learning how things worked in the colonies. Because he expected a siege at Fort Duquesne, his army was heavy with artillery. He brought with him four eight-inch howitzers, four twelve-pounders, six six-pounders, and fifteen Coehorn mortars.[4] He also had a significant amount of shot, shell, and ammunition. The sheer weight of the weapons required an extraordinary number of horses for movement. For example, each howitzer required nine horses; the twelve-pounder required seven horses; six horses to each wagon that carried the mortars; and each six-pounder had four to six horses. This amounted to hundreds of horses that consumed thousands of bushels of fodder. Although the locals had promised to provide an adequate number of horses and the necessary fodder, they did not.

Washington was only too familiar with the need for adequate transportation, food, and supplies. To move this vast quantity of arms, Braddock had the men construct a road as they moved; they completed about two miles a day. When the troops finally arrived at Fort Cumberland on May 14, Washington wrote that the march from Frederick Town had gone slowly and "I fear we shall remain some time for want of Horses and Carriages to convey our Baggage &ca over the Mountains; but more especially for want of Forage; as it cannot be imagin'd that so many Horses as we require, will be subsisted without [a great deal]."[5] He also feared the French were going to receive help from the Canadian Indians.

Fearing the permanent French presence at Fort Duquesne, the Ohio Valley Indians wanted to assist the British. Six chiefs arrived to parley. The Delaware Chief, Shingas, even provided a map of the fort. Sketched by Captain Robert Stobo, still a captive from the Great Meadows fiasco, the drawing had been smuggled out. Unfortunately the arrogant Braddock blew the opportunity to enlist the native aid which would prove so crucial in the future.

Shingas, speaking for all the tribes, asked Braddock for a promise to let them have sufficient grounds on which to live and hunt if the Indians helped the British expel the French. Braddock haughtily responded that only the English would live on the land. Again Shingas asked the question and added "that if they might not have Liberty To Live on the Land they would not Fight for it." Demonstrating the European's superior attitude for all things colonial that would soon prove so costly, Braddock replied that in that case he did not want or need their help. Humiliated and angry, all but eight of the Indians left, some of them to join the French.[6]

On May 29, in the midst of a severe drought, Braddock's force of more than 2,200 left Fort Cumberland. Their objective was over 110 miles away across mountains and through deep forests. A week into the journey, averaging only five miles a day, Braddock decided to split his forces. He would send out a "flying column" of lightly supplied troops with the supply train following. Washington, "sized wt vilt Fevers & Pns in my hd," for which he was given "Doctor Jas Powder," remained behind.[7] By July 9 Braddock was within ten miles of Fort Duquesne. Here Washington, riding on a saddle of pillows and "very weak and low," needing to stop frequently along the way due to a severe bout with dysentery joined the column. During the ensuing battle, again Washington would escape unscathed. He credited God and believed he had "been protected beyond all human probability."[8]

On July 9 Lieutenant Colonel Thomas Gage, commander of the Forty-Fourth Regiment, arrived with three hundred regulars at the crossing of the Monongahela about ten miles south of the Forks. After a scouting party announced they had seen signs of recent activity, they crossed. By early afternoon, Braddock, with all his wagons and supplies, had crossed. Suddenly Gage heard firing from the advance party and sent half his troops to investigate. Almost immediately they met fleeing troops who reported an attack by highly armed Indians. What followed was a disaster compounded by panic in the face of an unorthodox enemy.

Hit by fire from both sides, the colonial troops tried to form and fire. The Indians refused to present themselves as targets. Hiding behind trees and bushes and moving fast, they poured fire into their surprised enemy. Smoke clouded the vision as the retreating troops ran into those advancing with the wagons, supplies, and fifty female camp followers, all of which became a barrier to escape. In the confusion many died by friendly fire.[9] In a letter to his mother, Washington would decry the actions of the regular soldiers "who were struck with such a panick, that they behavd with more cowardice than it is possible to conceive."[10]

Racing to the front to bring order to chaos, Braddock quickly went down as the first of four horses was shot out from under him. Men fell all around him as the screams of the wounded and the war cries of the natives filled the air. After three hours of intense battle, Braddock received a mortal bullet wound in the back and tumbled from his fifth mount. Washington, now the only officer not dead or wounded, took command. He placed Braddock on a cart and began the long retreat back to Fort Cumberland. In a lucid moment, the dying general ordered Washington to return to Colonel Dunbar, commander of the remainder of his troops, and request provisions, medical supplies, and cover for the retreat.

Washington, still suffering the effects of his fever and diarrhea, rode all night and into the next morning. The night was so dark, and the forest so thick, his two guides had to grope "on the ground with their hands" to lead him. Many wounded were left to the mercy of the Indians. Their cries, screams, and moans would haunt Washington for years. Braddock lingered three days before succumbing to his wounds. Washington buried him along the recently constructed road. Wagons rolled over the unmarked grave so the Indians could not find it and desecrate his body. The devastated army took nine days to arrive at safety.[11]

The Virginians "behavd like Men, and died like Soldier's," wrote Washington to Dinwiddie on July 18. The British regulars, however, came in for a scathing indictment. They turned and "broke & run as Sheep before the Hounds, leavg the Artillery, Ammunition, Provision, and every individual thing we had with us a prey to the Enemy." This may have actually saved lives as the Indians did not pursue the fleeing soldiers across the Monongahela but ransacked their baggage and took all they could carry.[12]

After writing that reports of his death and "dying speech" were premature, Washington wrote his brother John, assuring him he was alive "by the miraculous care of Providence." Two horses were shot out from under him and four bullets pierced his coat, yet he remained unscathed. Years later in a reflective mood, he revised his journal to read, "death was levelling my companions on every side." Every other officer on horseback had been either killed or wounded.[13]

He reiterated this theme in a letter to a friend Robert Jackson. They were shamefully beaten by an inferior force who only wanted to "molest and disturb our March . . . but see the wondrous works of Providence! the uncertainty of Human things." Soon, the young Washington became the talk of the colonies.[14]

Several early accounts of Washington include a story told and recorded by Washington's adopted son, George Washington Parke Custis. He related how fifteen years after this battle, Washington and his friend and personal physician, Dr. Craik, were walking near where the Battle of Monongahela had taken place. There they met an aging Indian chief who remembered the battle. He recalled that when he first saw Washington astride his mount, and because he rode and fought like an Indian, it was believed he could not be British. The chief had ordered his braves to fire at Washington but "a power mightier far than we shielded you." Believing he was under the "special guardianship of the Great Spirit," they stopped shooting at him. The old chief prophesied that Washington would become the chief of nations and that "a people yet unborn will hail him as the founder of a mighty empire." Washington was "a particular favorite of heaven, and who could never die in battle," he added. Indeed, it would prove true that Washington would never be wounded in battle.[15]

Samuel Davies, a Presbyterian minister, praised him from the pulpit as "that heroic Youth Col. Washington, who I cannot but hope Providence has hitherto preserved in so signal a Manner for some important Service to his Country." Many believed he would eventually be the commander of Virginia's troops, a hope held by Washington himself, and sought to serve under him. The Virginia Assembly met to discuss the matter.[16]

Braddock's defeat taught Washington many a military lesson. He was appalled at the lack of discipline in the regular British forces. Trained to fight in ranks under close supervision, they were helpless when conditions on the battlefield changed. They lacked initiative and confidence and their poor fire discipline caused many casualties.

Another important lesson learned was that inadequate logistical support caused both loss of life and victory. Heavy weapons and baggage meant horses or mules that required fodder. Troops needed adequate food, arms, and powder. On the positive, Washington learned that his colonial troops could fight with the best European troops. Highly critical of the British troops, he praised his Virginia militia. They adapted well to the hit-and-run style of fighting practiced by the Indians.

Washington also recognized the need for intelligence. Braddock failed to deploy adequate scouts and his forward troops were surprised by the advancing enemy. Knowledge of the enemy and his movements became a priority. Washington took note of this and it would prove decisive in his future battles.

On August 14, from Mount Vernon, he assured his anxious mother he would do all in his power not to go to the Ohio again, "but if the Command is press'd upon me by the genl voice of the Country, and offerd upon such terms as can't be objected against, it would reflect eternal dishonour upon me to refuse it."[17]

Puffed up by his popularity, Washington believed he had

sufficient clout to dictate terms for his command. He refused to attend the Assembly meeting to discuss the future of the militia because he "coud not get a command upon such terms as I shoud care to accept, as I must confess I never will quit my Family, injure my Fortune, and (above all) impair my health to run the risque of such Changes and Viscissitudes as I have done; but shall now expect if I am employed again to have something certain."[18]

Washington's demand, "which ignorance and inexperience made me overlook before," was to have a say in selecting his officers. Since the "unfortunate Chief" of a losing battle receives the blame, he should also get to choose and train those upon whom his reputation rests. In addition, he needed a "small military chest" to carry out his orders. Finally, he did not want to again be in the position of not having sufficient horses and wagons to cross the frontier. He left the door open, however, to assuming command. He wrote that although this letter sounded like he was declining any option of serving, his real meaning was "entirely different." He did not want it to appear that he was making demands and asking for the job at the same time.

Although London did not recognize his skills, the Assembly of Virginia and Governor Dinwiddie did: at the end of August 1755, Washington was appointed colonel and commander of the Virginia Regiment.[19]

He immediately began practicing the lessons he'd learned. "Remember that it is the actions, and not the commission, that

makes the officer," he admonished, an officer under his command, "and that there is more expected of him than the title."
The militia as a whole could expect him "to observe the strictest
discipline through the whole economy of my behavior."[20] He
would not be biased in his actions, but be extremely fair, reward
merit, and administer justice evenhandedly.

Discipline was severe by our contemporary standards. If an
enlisted man swore or used an "oath of execration" he was given
twenty-five lashes on the spot. No court martial needed. For shirk-
ing of duty or visiting one of the off-limits "tippling houses or gin
shops," a soldier received fifty lashes in front of his fellow men. If
the men trained hard and behaved themselves, the colonel would
provide them with "four gallons of rum made into punch" each
day. To discourage desertion Washington threatened hanging. (In
1757 the Assembly did permit capital punishment for deserters
in a military code.) Washington did hang two deserters from his
forty-foot-high gallows. He decided on this punishment rather
than the firing squad because "it conveyed much more terror to
others." "Discipline is the soul of the army," he wrote on another
occasion. Even officers were not immune from punishment. To
one captain he wrote, "There are continual complaints to me of
the misbehavior of your Wife, who I am told sows sedition among
the men and is chief of every mutiny." If the officer did not drive
her out of camp, Washington promised to do so when he arrived.
He also sacked an officer for cheating at cards.[21]

By the fall of 1758, the twenty-six-year-old Washington
was suffering from dysentery and returned to Mount Vernon to
recover. By March he was still so ill he considered retirement,

and again threatened to resign his commission, retire from public life, and concentrate on his health and business. In reply to his letter regarding this, Colonel John Stanwix wrote that perhaps Washington should reconsider his options, since a large force of perhaps seven thousand men was coming from England. They would possibly be going to take Fort Duquesne and would need leadership. This seemed to improve Washington's spirit and health. About a week later he wrote a cousin that he was regaining his health.[22]

Another event that might have improved Washington's health was his having met the wealthiest widow in Virginia—Martha Custis. Good-humoredly, she described herself as "a fine healthy girl." She had dark hair, hazel eyes, beautiful teeth (important in those days), and was "agreeably plump." Described as being pretty and perky, as steady as a clock, as cheerful as a cricket, and as busy as a bee, she was a prize Washington sought. Because Martha burned their letters after his death, we know little of their courtship. Martha's grandson, George Washington Parkes Custis, told the romantic tale of their chance meeting at a friend's house: Washington had planned only to stay for dinner but after meeting, he and Martha talked all night. When he left in the morning, they were engaged.[23]

Washington read his resignation speech in Annapolis (1817).

Washington taking command of the American army under
the old elm at Cambridge (1906).

Charles Wilson Peale

Washington wearing his Colonel's uniform of the Virginia
Regiment from the French and Indian War (1772).

F O U R

Road to Revolution

It has been . . . destiny that has thrown me upon this service.

— GEORGE WASHINGTON

IN 1757 WILLIAM Pitt became the new secretary of state in England and decided to prosecute the war against the French much more aggressively. To this end he sent three generals to the colonies. Major General Jeffrey Amherst was in charge of taking Fort Louisburg in Nova Scotia. Major General James Abercromby, aided by Brigadier General George Augustus Howe, would concentrate on Fort Ticonderoga located along the Hudson River. Brigadier General John Forbes would become Washington's leader in the attempt at Fort Duquesne.

Forbes did not have a great opinion of colonial officers. Recognizing that Washington knew the terrain, he asked him to lead the Virginia troops. Washington immediately made two recommendations. The first was to acquire Indian allies. Their experience at fighting the French and other Indian tribes, coupled with an intimate knowledge of the area, meant the natives would make choice allies. Despite Forbes's best efforts, however, the Indians refused to support the English. Washington's other suggestion, to again attack using the Braddock Road, was rejected out of hand.

Forbes decided to take a more direct route to Fort Duquesne, from Shippensburg to Raystown in southwestern Pennsylvania. He wanted to forge a road and construct forts along the more than eighty-mile stretch through the forests of western Pennsylvania. Although he knew it would take longer, the conservative Forbes wanted the forts as fallback positions in case of attack. Washington was unhappy about this choice.

Unable to convince Forbes, who was aware of provincial politics, Washington went over his head to the newly appointed governor of Virginia, Francis Fauquier. Washington pleaded with him to stop the expedition and consider the Braddock road. "I said, and did every thing to avert a [*erasure*] that seemd to forebode our manifest Ruin," he wrote; "the thoughts of opening a Road 100 Miles in length—over Mountains almost inaccessable, at this advanced Season, when there is already a good Road made," made no military sense to him.[1]

Seeking additional support, Washington wrote to Speaker John Robinson. Washington argued that Forbes was under the influence of an "evil Geni" and they were duped by the Pennsylvanian faction who wanted profit more than victory. He believed "nothing now but a miracle can bring this Campaigne to a happy issue."[2] Still, he did not complain when appointed colonel and given command over the advance division to make the assault upon the fort.

Washington also disliked the fact that Pennsylvania merchants, rather than Virginians, would get the profit from outfitting the expedition. Although this northern route looked shorter, "[it] wou'd require so much time as to blast our otherwise well grounded hopes of striking the long wishd for, and Important Stroke this Season," he wrote Henry Bouquet, the commander in the field. Braddock's road was well used and in good shape and they would make better time, he argued. Despite Washington's best efforts, Forbes's decision was final.[3]

Writing his memoirs in 1784, long after the Revolutionary War, Washington referenced an incident during this campaign in which he believed his life "was in as much jeopardy as it had ever been before or since." The skirmish took place at Loyalhanna River, nearly halfway to Fort Duquesne. Although accounts of the incident vary, just prior to sunset a French raiding party attacked the troops guarding the outlying livestock. Hearing musket fire, Forbes sent Lieutenant Colonel George Mercer out with a few hundred troops. As the firing escalated, Forbes ordered Washington into the fray with a few hundred more. Smoke filled the ever-darkening sky and amid the confusion of battle it was difficult to distinguish friend from foe. Suddenly, Washington realized his troops were exchanging fire with those of Mercer. Disregarding his own safety and placing himself in the line of fire, Washington raced between the two lines, and wielding his sword he pushed up the weapons of his unit, forcing them to fire in the air. News of his bravery soon spread throughout the land.[4]

Ten miles from Fort Duquesne, the exhausted British and colonials heard a tremendous explosion. When Washington arrived at the fort on November 25, 1758, he found nothing but ashes. Ultimately the demise of Fort Duquesne did not depend upon which route was taken, but upon a British treaty with the Iroquois. A month earlier the Treaty of Easton had been concluded, under the terms of which the British agreed not to expand permanent settlements in the Ohio Valley. Thus control of the hunting grounds was ceded to the natives and France lost its local support. Afraid they could not withstand Forbes's troops after the desertion of Indian allies, French Captain Francois Lignery did what he had to: after saving the cannons and munitions, he burned the fort to the ground. He also planted barrels of gunpowder to ensure total destruction. He and his troops escaped by canoe up the Allegheny to safety.

What Washington felt at seeing the ruin of Fort Duquesne and realizing the campaign was over, we do not know. The previous four years spent in this specific area had changed and molded his life. In 1754, just east of where he now stood, he narrowly escaped being shot and almost drowned in a freezing river. A year later at Fort Necessity he was defeated by the French and admitted to the assassination of a French officer—an act that provoked a war. Along Braddock's Road he had two horses shot out from under him while his jacket absorbed four bullets more. Finally, just a few days previously, he'd risked his life to prevent his troops being killed by friendly fire.

Yet he survived, prospered, and—due to his newfound fame—
would win election to the House of Burgesses. Washington would
now return to his beloved Mount Vernon to marry his betrothed,
Martha Custis. The ceremony took place on January 6, 1759,
at her home on White House Plantation in New Kent County,
Virginia. As a result of this marriage, Washington was now one of
the wealthiest men in Virginia.[5]

Martha was a constant source of strength and comfort to her
husband; she was the ballast in his life that kept him on course
and steady, the rock on whom he always leaned. During the long
military campaigns of the Revolution, she often joined him and
shared in his hardships. Even when Washington was being criticized by military or political rivals, no one spoke badly of her or
of their relationship.

After his retirement from the Virginia Regiment in December
1758, Washington settled down to expanding his plantation at
Mount Vernon and raising his new family. The widowed Martha
came with two children from her previous marriage: John Parke
Custis, called Jackie, was five, and Martha Parke Custis, nicknamed Patsy, was three (Suffering from epilepsy, Patsy died at age
seventeen). Washington became their legal guardian. Under his
management, Mount Vernon grew to nearly six thousand acres,
with hundreds of slaves. Initially growing the popular Virginia
crop of tobacco, in 1766 Washington switched to growing the
more profitable wheat and corn; wheat could be sold domesti-
cally whereas tobacco was exported and therefore subject to not

only the whims of international trade but also British taxation. Although primarily engaged in running his various enterprises and caring for his family, Washington assumed a seat in the House of Burgesses in February 1759.

With the Treaty of Paris in 1763, the French and Indian—or Seven Years'—War ended. The war had cost dearly both in lives and treasure and the British government was seriously in debt. The Crown needed to raise funds—and what better way than taxation? Since part of the war had been fought in the colonies and British troops were still stationed there, it seemed only right for Parliament to make the colonists share in this tax burden. Thus in 1765, the Stamp Act, forcing a tax on all written documents, was enacted. Preachers were unhappy since their sermons were circulated in pamphlet form. Lawyers were forced to add a stamp to all legal papers. Even newspapers and playing cards came under the hated tax, angering both newspaper owners and the sailors who gambled in the grog shops.

Washington also was not happy. In September 1765, he wrote Martha's uncle, Francis Dandridge, in London. "The Stamp Act Imposed on the Colonies," he assured Francis, had angered the colonists, "who look upon this unconstitutional method of Taxation as a direful attack upon their Liberties, & loudly exclaim against the Violation—what may be the result of this . . . ill judgd Measures, I will not undertake to determine." Due to mounting pressure, Parliament repealed the Stamp Act in March 1766, but at the same time it pronounced the Declaratory Act. This asserted the British retained the right to levy taxes "in all cases whatsoever" over their colonies.[6]

The following year Parliament attempted a new revenue-producing tax—the Townshend Acts—imposing taxes on imported goods from Britain such as lead, paper, paint, glass, and tea. Whereas the Stamp Act involved internal taxes, or those originating within the colonies, the new act involved external taxes on goods coming from outside the colonies. In protest, merchants, especially in the port cities of Boston, New York, and Philadelphia, boycotted the importation of British goods.

In Virginia, Washington wrote his friend George Mason that "our lordly Masters in Great Britain will be satisfied with nothing less than the deprication of American freedom . . . derived from our Ancestors." The use of arms to defend this freedom was justified, but only as "the last resource."[7] When the Virginia House of Burgesses voted a resolution stating that Parliament had no right to tax Virginians without their consent or to ship colonial protestors to England for trial, the royally appointed Governor Lord Botetourt dissolved the House.

Again, British merchants hurt by the boycotting of their goods pressured Parliament to repeal these duties. In April 1770, at the request of the new prime minister, Lord North, Parliament repealed all the taxes except the tax on tea. Not wanting to appear to buckle under pressure, North kept the tea tax just to let the protestors know who was in control; the news arrived in the colonies about a month after the infamous Boston Massacre occurred on April 5, 1770. North's policy was further extended by the Tea Act of 1773, allowing the East India Company to monopolize the tea trade and ship tea directly to the colonists. Protest again broke out in the port cities. Tax collectors were tarred and feathered and run out of town. In December 1773, in an event remembered as the Boston Tea Party, a group calling themselves the Sons of Liberty further escalated the crisis by tossing tons of taxed tea into Boston Harbor.

The British response to all of this was the Coercive Acts. Passed six months after the Boston Tea Party, they were quickly labeled the Intolerable Acts. Punitive in nature, the laws closed the port of Boston until the tea lost in the Tea Party was paid for, allowed for the quartering of troops at colonial expense, replaced elected Massachusetts officials with those from England, and provided for the extradition of suspected rebels to other colonies or even England for trial. This was the final straw for many in the colonies. In Virginia, the royally appointed governor, Lord John Dunmore, dissolved the House after it condemned these acts. Events were now in play that could only lead to violence.

The colonists began planning their response to the outrage; and the First Continental Congress convened in Philadelphia from September 5 to October 26, 1774. The meeting was attended by representatives from all the colonies except Georgia. Washington, Richard Henry Lee, and Patrick Henry were among Virginia's seven delegates. The fifty-six members of the Continental Congress agreed to boycott trade with Britain and to meet again the next May to assess the progress. Individual colonies began to train militia and stockpile arms and ammunition.

On April 19, 1775, British General Thomas Gage sent seven hundred redcoats from Boston to confiscate a cache of arms in Lexington and Concord. Under the command of Lieutenant Colonel Francis Smith, they were also to arrest colonial leaders

Samuel Adams and John Hancock. The two men were warned of the enemy's approach, though, by a silversmith named Paul Revere.

As the sun rose, about sixty patriots, led by John Parker, confronted the advance party of the British troops under the command of Captain John Pitcairn. "Lay down your arms," roared Pitcairn. As the militia grudgingly disbanded, "the shot heard round the world" rang out. No one knows who fired it but soon the British were discharging fixed volleys into the militia. Seven militia went down as the others ran for cover. Then, moving on to Concord, the redcoats destroyed some gunpowder and began the sixteen-mile return to Boston. Colonials, fighting Indian style from behind stone walls and trees, turned the day into a running brawl. At the end of the long, exhausting retreat, British casualties numbered 73 killed and 174 wounded; the American toll was 49 dead and 39 wounded. The war that would lead to American independence had begun.[8]

On May 10, 1775, the Second Continental Congress convened in Philadelphia. Washington arrived the day before, dressed in his red and blue colonel's uniform from the French and Indian War. Congress realized that one of the most important issues they faced was the military defense of the colonies. The British were in Boston and were expected to react to the skirmishes at Lexington and Concord. Militias were forming throughout the territories but needed weapons—and a leader. George Washington was an obvious choice. Although a Virginian, he was well known among all the colonies, had experience, and, at least outwardly, affected a disinterest in the position.

Washington was also a realist. Although he had stated many times he did not want war with England, he was prepared for it. After hearing about what had happened in Boston he wrote a letter, dated May 31, 1775, to his friend George Fairfax. "Unhappy it is though to reflect, that a Brother's Sword has been sheathed in a Brother's breast, and that, the once happy and peaceful plains of America are either to be drenched with Blood, or Inhabited by Slaves. Sad alternative! But can a virtuous Man hesitate in his choice?"[9]

Some have criticized an overeager Washington for seeking command. If he was not "applying" for the job as commander in chief, why did he wear his uniform? Why did he purchase military books and a silk sash traditionally worn by officers? Here again we observe the mystery that was Washington. On the one hand was his ambition, usually hidden beneath a rather formal exterior, yet occasionally revealing itself for all to see. On the other his humility and graciousness, acquired in his efforts to become a gentleman, forbade him from appearing too eager to grasp position.

Perhaps he considered the alternatives for leadership. There was John Hancock, one of the wealthiest men in New England. There was also the veteran from the French and Indian War, Artemas Ward, who now commanded the militia in Boston. Also available was the professional soldier Charles Lee, who had served with Braddock and in European commands before permanently moving to the colonies in 1773. Each of these possible choices had their advocates and factions and eagerly sought the position. Perhaps in his heart Washington realized he was the only man who could unite the colonies and who had enough experience and drive to command the untrained men in the coming war.

When John Adams, the scholarly attorney from Massachusetts, rose to speak on his behalf, Washington discreetly left the room to give the delegates the opportunity to talk freely about him. Adams declared that the army at Boston needed leadership and military supplies and needed them quickly—before they deserted. "I had no hesitation to declare that I had but one Gentleman in my Mind for that important command," the portly Adams recalled addressing Congress, "and that was a Gentleman from Virginia who was among Us and very well known to all of Us, a Gentleman whose Skill and Experience as an Officer, whose independent fortune, great Talents and excellent universal Character, would command the Approbation of all America, and unite the cordial Exertions of all the Colonies better than any other Person in the Union." Congress agreed.[10]

On June 15 the Congress unanimously appointed Washington commander in chief and on the next day he accepted, stating:

Mr. President: Tho' I am truly sensible of the high Honour done me in this Appointment, yet I feel great distress from a consciousness that my abilities and Military experience may not be equal to the extensive and important Trust: However, as the Congress desires if I will enter upon the momentous duty, and exert every power I Possess in their service & for the Support of the glorious Cause: I beg they will accept my most cordial thanks for this distinguished testimony of their Approbation.[11]

Two days later Washington wrote Martha of his appointment and informed her of the need to hasten to Boston. He'd used "every endeavor in my power to avoid it," he confessed, lamenting his absence from her and expressing his own personal feeling of inadequacy, "its being a trust too great for my Capacity." Yet he also wrote, "it has been a kind of destiny, that has thrown me upon this Service." His character and conscience would not allow him to refuse; "I shall rely therefore, confidently, on that Providence, which has heretofore preservd & been bountiful to me, not doubting but that I shall return safe to you in the fall." He finished this letter by commenting that he would have his will made before he set out.[12]

Ever the realist, Washington knew what his new role might cost him. The day "I enter upon the command of the American armies," he confided to Patrick Henry, "I date my fall, and the ruin of my reputation." Still, he was willing to sacrifice his personal fortune, his reputation and even his life in the service of his country. "I can answer but for three things," he assured fellow House member Burwell Bassett, "a firm belief of the justice of our Cause—close attention in the prosecution of it—and the strictest Integrety—If these cannot supply the places of Ability & Experience, the cause will suffer."[13]

FIVE

Commander in Chief

An Army without Order, Regularity & Discipline, is no better
than a Commission'd Mob.

—GEORGE WASHINGTON

ON JUNE 23, 1775, the new commander in chief left
Philadelphia to join the troops in Boston. "I go fully trusting . . .
Providence," he scribbled to Martha minutes before leaving. Along
the way he had to deal with cheering crowds and fawning officials. In New York he found not only crowds of well-wishers but
also faced loyalists, who numbered a third of the country.[1] While
in New York, desperate for any news from Boston, Washington
intercepted, opened, and read a letter addressed to Congress.
He discovered a major battle had taken place on June 17 (now
called the Battle of Bunker Hill). His trip took on a new sense

of urgency. Arriving on July 2, exhausted from the "excessive Civilities" shown him along the way, he attempted to inspect the enemy positions but a downpour and subsequent fog prevented him from seeing much until the next day.[2]

In the fight at Boston, British troops under the command of William Howe had attacked and ultimately replaced the entrenched American forces on the Charlestown Peninsula, comprised of Bunker Hill and Breed's Hill. Across the Charles River was the city of Boston, under British control; to its east lay Cambridge. Although it lasted only a few hours, Bunker Hill proved the ragged continentals could stand up to the disciplined redcoats. Twice they repulsed the British attack. Yet on the third assault, the British chased the Americans—now low on ammunition—off the hill and the peninsula. Howe's troops suffered over 1,000 casualties out of 2,500, while the colonists lost 441. Both sides learned valuable lessons about the other. The colonists discovered the British were vulnerable but exhibited a bulldog mentality. They did not quit. The British discovered the colonists were serious in their desire for liberty and would not run when confronted, even by a superior force. Both knew a long and bloody war lay ahead.

The next months were crucial to the success of the American forces. Washington quickly discovered he was in a different situation than when he served under British authority. Although he had combat experience, most of his men did not. He was tasked with building an army from scratch and doing so within sight of an enemy that might attack at any time. He needed to make fundamental decisions, including the design of uniforms, the digging of latrines, and the providing of straw for the men to sleep on. There was also the changed perception of command. Washington, the wealthy, slave-owning gentleman, who was used to giving orders and having them obeyed, was about to encounter an entirely different sort of colonial citizen.

Upon his arrival in Boston, Washington was dismayed to find "a numerous army of Provincials under very little command, discipline, or order." On the other hand, "I found our Enemy . . . strongly Intrenching," he informed his brother Samuel. He estimated the British strength at ten to twelve thousand. His troops numbered between sixteen and eighteen thousand, although that included the sick and absent.[3] Both sides were content to take a defensive posture. Washington's initial mission was to count his troops, evaluate their leadership, physical condition, and begin the discipline needed to whip this ragtag band into some semblance of an army.

Two days after his arrival, July 4, 1775, Washington laid the groundwork for the Army of the United States. In a two-page document, he addressed three of the main obstacles in establishing the new army: the need to create a unified army, establish a chain of command, and demand that officers care for and take responsibility for their men's condition. Each of these principles had to be ingrained into the mentality of a people who saw themselves primarily as residents of a specific colony—free individuals under the authority of no man—and who had no experience with an officer class, one that had both punitive authority over them and responsibility for their welfare.

To establish a chain of command, Washington recognized

the appointment of four major generals by the Continental Congress—Artemus Ward, Charles Lee, Philip Schuyler, and Israel Putnam, or "old Put," as he was affectionately known. Other officers appointed by their respective colonies continued in their current rank. To shift allegiance from individual colonies and create a sense of unity, pay and service of the soldiers now came under the authority of the Continental Congress. "They are now the Troops of the UNITED PROVINCES of North America," read the orders, "and it is hoped that all Distinctions of Colonies will be laid aside; so that one and the same Spirit may animate the whole."[4] This particular goal would plague commanders and presidents for nearly the next century.

His second general orders "required and expected that exact discipline be observed, and due Subordination prevail thro' the whole Army." Recognizing character and discipline were interrelated, he added, "The General most earnestly requires, and expects, a due observance of those articles of war . . . which forbid profane cursing, swearing and drunkenness." For spiritual development he expected "all Officers and Soldiers, not engaged on actual duty, a punctual attendance on divine Service, to implore the blessings of heaven upon the means used for our safety and defence."[5] Six weeks later in a subsequent general orders he expounded, "Disobedience of orders is amongst the first and most atrocious of all military Crimes."[6]

He advised a newly appointed colonel to "be strict in your discipline; to require nothing unreasonable of your officers and men, but see that whatever is required be punctually complied with." Each man was to be rewarded or punished based upon his own actions without partiality. If a man complained, "hear his complaints; if well founded, redress them; if otherwise discourage them, in order to prevent frivolous ones." Orders were to be "plain and precise" and copies should be made to back up all decisions. The colonel should be "easy and condescending in your deportment to your officers, but not too familiar, lest you subject yourself to a want of that respect, which is necessary to support a proper command."[7]

Noticing a foul stench in the air from overflowing latrines and the general filth of the men, he addressed these concerns in his general orders. "Take care that Necessarys [latrines] be provided in the Camps and frequently filled up to prevent their being offensive and unhealthy." Officers were responsible for their men's hygiene, especially to make sure the men "have straw to lay on."[8]

Apparently the men also were concerned with cleanliness. "The General does not mean to discourage the practice of bathing," included the general orders of August 22, "but he expressly forbids, any persons doing it, at or near the Bridge in Cambridge, where it has been observed and complained of, that many Men, lost to all sense of decency and common modesty, are running about naked upon the Bridge, whilst Passengers, and even Ladies of the first fashion in the neighbourhood, are passing over it."[9]

The egalitarian nature of the troops from Massachusetts especially confounded the aristocratic Virginian. They generally elected their officers and could easily "fire" them if not pleased with their orders. Discipline consequently was lax. He cashiered several officers for cowardice. In the absence of actual combat, many felt no need to be vigilant on guard duty. "It is among the most difficult tasks I ever undertook in my life to induce these people to believe that there is . . . danger till the Bayonet is pushing at their Breasts," he complained to Richard Henry Lee. This lax attitude proceeded from "an unaccountable kind of stupidity in the lower class of these people, which believe me prevails but too generally among the Officers of the Massachusetts part of the Army." The Virginia planter was getting to know the Yankee farmer.[10]

On July 20, 1775, Congress recommended a day of public fasting and prayer throughout the colonies to "implore the Divine benediction on our country; that any further shedding of blood may be averted; and that the calamities with which we are afflicted may be removed."[11] The recommendation was designed to not only seek divine protection but also to unite the country in a common goal. Throughout the war, Congress recognized the need to foster common faith and religious observances to mold the colonists into one people. Given that Americans were a religiously inspired people, faith was key to shaping the fledgling nation just as it was key to shaping an army.

Still, it would never be an easy task. The militias were a motley collection of farmers, fishermen, and mechanics from distinct regions, who carried a variety of weapons lacking uniformity of caliber or bullet molds. Clothing, too, varied. Some were dressed in threadbare homespun shirts; others wore buckskins with cowhide shoes. Most had breeches tied below the knees and buckled shoes. Headgear also varied. Coonskin caps, beaver or felt hats, round brimmed hats, or perhaps the most prevalent, the tricorne, were all in style. A young surgeon recalled seeing Washington for the first time, describing him as dressed in a "blue coat with buff colored facings, a rich epaulette on each shoulder, buff under dress, and an elegant small sword; a black cockade in his hat." Physically he was easily distinguished because "his personal appearance is truly noble and majestic being tall and well proportioned."[12] He stood out, too, because he was one of the few impressively dressed figures on the field.

Sometime in August a contingent of fourteen hundred men, carrying the famous long rifles, arrived from Pennsylvania and Delaware. Distinguished also by their comfortable and functional dress—linen or buckskin hunting shirts belted at the waist and ending at mid-thigh, lower legs covered with leggings for protection, feet shod with moccasins—they presented a formidable appearance. Since powder and shot had to be carried for long distances by these frontiersmen, they used a smaller caliber than the musket. New Englanders, like John Adams, had never seen such weapons. Writing Abigail, he described "a peculiar kind of [Firearm ca]ll'd a Rifle—it has circular or [...]Grooves within the Barrell, and carries a Ball, with great Exactness to great Distances. They are the most accurate Marksmen in the World."[13]

Although accurate—they could hit a target seven inches in diameter from 250 yards while moving at a trot—they took longer to load and fire. A trained soldier could fire three shots with his musket to one from the long rifle. Another disadvantage was its inability to be fitted for a bayonet. Still, being accurate at twice the range of the musket, they were excellent for sniper fire. Many British soldiers, careless enough to expose their heads at what would normally be considered a safe range, were picked off.

British officers were the most highly prized targets. Most troops had the "Brown Bess" musket, so named because of the color of the stock. Notoriously inaccurate at distances over one hundred yards, the barrel was short and unrifled; it was designed for European-style tactics—troops lined up facing each other at one hundred yards or so and fired away until one side broke and ran. A soldier merely pointed the weapon at the opposing army and pulled the trigger, usually closing his eyes to prevent injury as the spark ignited the powder. Speed of loading and amount of fire was the key. Once the opposing force turned and ran, the other side could chase them and bayonet the stragglers.

Weaponry handicapped the British but so did the customs of its professional military. Unlike the superlative British navy, which had a system of promotion based on competency and merit, army officers bought their commissions. The higher the rank, the higher the price; competency had nothing to do with rank. Once purchased, these commissions became the property of the officer, who could sell it to yet another. Price also varied by the type of unit. General officers were usually titled. Many who entered at the bottom officer ranks, sometimes as young as fifteen, were from the middle class and hoped to improve their social status through battlefield promotions.

Enlisted troops typically came from the very bottom of the social order. Occasionally jails were emptied to fill a unit. Many did not actually volunteer but were tricked to "take the king's shilling." If a recruiter could fool the victim into taking the shilling, he was in the army. One favorite ruse was for the recruiter to visit the countryside and offer free drinks to innocent and unsophisticated local youths. After a couple of pints, the sergeant put a shilling into the mug of ale. As the unsuspecting, probably tipsy, youngster drained his mug, the shilling would go into his mouth. Since he had "taken the shilling" he was under the authority of the military. Thus the glass-bottomed mug was born: even a drunk could see if there was a shilling at the bottom.

Given these unwise practices, why did the British troops fight so well? After all, they were looked down upon by society, had forfeited most of their rights, and were daily exposed to physical hardships that could result in death. What was their motivation? Why did they acquit themselves well in battle, as even the colonists admitted? The reasons are known by the brotherhood of arms through all ages. The army provided food, however poor, and a uniform. A soldier was part of a unit that ate, slept, trained, and suffered together. Although discipline was harsh—floggings were common even for minor infractions—each man felt connected to his comrades. A universal military truism is that men do not fight for some great cause such as king and country; these are rather abstract ideas. Instead they fight and endure the hardships of battle for something much more obvious—their messmates, those who stand with them on the left and right. This sense of camaraderie or *esprit de corps* must exist in an effective fighting force and it did among the British troops in colonial America.[14]

The colonials had yet to match the British in spirit or in materiel. Washington was as appalled by the lack of basic military equipment as he was the lack of discipline. He was powerless to remedy the situation. "I find myself embarrassed for Want of a military Chest," he complained to Congress. "I must therefore request that Money may be forwarded as soon as possible." Tents made from worn-out sails provided little shelter. The disparities in clothing and equipment among the colonial troops also troubled him. The ragged clothing of the Massachusetts troops especially concerned him. He requested ten thousand hunting shirts not only to clothe the men but also to "abolish those Provincial Distinctions which lead to Jealousy and Dissatisfaction."[15] Washington was realizing how desperately he needed a professional army.

Initially, he bought time. He was content to play defense by strengthening his position and preventing the enemy from receiving supplies. In time he decided to force the issue. To open a second front and bottle up the troops in Boston, Congress decided he should attack the British in Canada. Washington agreed and sent Colonel Benedict Arnold to Quebec. Arnold was to block resupply of the British via the Saint Lawrence and to ascertain the sentiments of the Canadians. Rumors abounded that they, too, were unhappy with British rule. Arnold encouraged the Canadians to join their brothers in the south, to rise up and throw off the yoke of tyranny imposed upon them by the Crown. Washington gave specific orders to pay for supplies taken, respect the Catholic faith, and to keep the men from looting or plundering from either the Canadians or the Indians. It was open season, however, if they came upon any British supplies. Unfortunately the expedition was poorly planned and Arnold was wounded after failing to take Quebec.

Washington's most pressing problem was the looming end of the citizen-soldiers' enlistment. Those from Connecticut and

Rhode Island had signed on until December 1, and both cajol-
ing and appeals to patriotism fell on deaf ears. The others would
leave on January 1, 1776. The need to return home and provide
for their families took precedence over patriotic duties. Powder
was also running low. Knowing the enemy was aware of his predicament forced Washington to act. In a desperate gamble to
bring this situation to a conclusion before his army melted away
or the enemy received reinforcements, he petitioned Congress for
the authority to attack Boston.

On October 15, Benjamin Franklin and two congressional
appointees met with Washington. They agreed on some issues—
like not permitting blacks to enlist in the army and on raising a
new army of twenty thousand—but dithered on the plan to attack.
A despondent and perhaps cynical Washington wrote his secretary Joseph Reed, "What an astonishing thing it is, that those who
are employed to sign the Continental Bills should not be able or
Inclined to do it as fast as they are wanted. They will proove the
destruction of the Army if they are not more attentive and dili-
gent. Such a dearth of Publick Spirit & want of Virtue; such stock
jobbing, and fertility in all the low arts to obtain advantages, of
one kind or another." The attitude of the troops also frustrated
him. "The Connecticut troops will not be prevailed upon to stay
longer than their term . . . and such a dirty mercenary Spirit per-
vades the whole that I should not at all be surprizd at any disaster
that may happen."[16]

Three days before Christmas, with his ill-clothed and poorly
housed troops freezing, Washington received approval for the
attack. At this point the Connecticut militia had left and the

remaining militia would in a week's time. Lacking artillery, trained troops, and supplies, an attack appeared impossible. In January, Washington again wrote Reed and confessed that the weight of command was wearing on him. He admitted he wished he was a simple rifleman in the ranks and not in command. In a very poignant line he bared his soul, revealed his sense of destiny, and demonstrated strength of character. He would have been happier, he wrote, "if I could have justified the Measure to Posterity, & my own Conscience, had retir'd to the back Country, & livd in a Wig-wam."[17]

As 1775 came to a close Washington faced disaster. Congress had authorized an army of twenty thousand, but less than half were recruited. Massive troop loss due to expired enlistments and a lack of new recruits made him a general with no army. Worse, this troop departure took place under the watchful view of the enemy. What would Howe make of it all?

January 1, 1776, was a momentous day in the history of the Continental Army. On this day "the new- army, which, in every point of View is entirely Continental" was born. No longer under the authority of their colonial leadership, the troops were now commanded by Washington under the authority of Congress. No one understood this better than the commander in chief. On this day he issued the first general orders to this newly minted continental army.[18]

Washington knew he was fashioning a culture as well as a fighting force. A "Spirit of emulation" must pervade the army; "without such a Spirit, few Officers have ever arrived to any degree of Reputation, nor did any Army ever become formidable:

His Excellency hopes that the Importance of the great Cause we are engaged in, will be deeply impressed upon every Man's mind, and wishes it to be considered that an Army without Order, Regularity & Discipline, is no better than a Commission'd Mob." Leadership was to "endeavor by all the Skill and Discipline in our power, to acquire that knowledge and conduct, which is necessary in War—Our men are brave and good; Men who with pleasure it is observed, are addicted with fewer Vices than are commonly found in Armies; but it is Subordination & Discipline (the Life and Soul of an Army) which next under providence, is to make us formidable to our enemies, honorable in ourselves, and respected in the world; and herein is to be shewn the Goodness of the Officer."[19]

Washington made it clear his desire was to see an army that willingly obeyed clear, direct, and explained orders. Obedience brought rewards with promotion, and disobedience brought public punishment. He solicited the advice and counsel of junior officers, yet input had to follow the regular chain of command for implementation. Although he would receive recommendations for the appointment of officers, only Congress could authorize their appointments.[20]

Frustrated by inactivity, on January 24 he lamented to Congress, "No man upon Earth wishes more ardently to destroy the Nest in Boston than I do—no person would be willing to goe to greater lengths than I shall to accomplish it. But if we have neither Powder to Bombard with, not Ice to pass on, we shall be in no better situation than we have been in all the year—we shall be worse, because their works are stronger."

Washington desired to attack the British before they could be resupplied and fortified by sea but had neither the trained nor armed troops necessary to accomplish this. He called a counsel of his commanders to seek advice. Overwhelmingly they counseled caution and suggested fortifying the high ground of Dorchester Heights overlooking Boston. This hill, about 150 feet above sea level and reachable only by treacherous and icy paths, made this feat difficult. If successful, however, it provided a field of fire covering both the city of Boston and the British fleet. Washington hoped the British would charge up the hill as they had at Bunker Hill. This time, however, he would make better preparations to welcome them.[21]

The question of canon illustrates the type of predicament that often beset Washington. Colonel Henry Knox, a fleshy 280-pound Boston bookseller turned artillery colonel, had secured cannon from the captured Fort Ticonderoga in upstate New York. It took fifty-six days for his troops to sled the sixty cannon and mortars to within twenty miles of Cambridge, a journey of about three hundred miles. Despite this extraordinary feat, no one had experience with aligning and firing cannon. Powder for practice was practically nonexistent. Washington knew he had to make other arrangements.

Preparation for defending the Heights began immediately. Barrels filled with dirt and stone to roll down upon the expected uphill assault were readied. Movable breastworks were also set up for protection. Medical supplies were gathered for the expected casualties. "These are the preparations for blood and slaughter!" a field surgeon later wrote, "Gracious God! If it be determined in thy Providence that thousands of our fellow creatures shall this day be slain, let thy wrath be appeased, and in mercy grant, that victory be on the side of our suffering, bleeding, country."[22]

For three nights Washington used the little powder he had to provide a diversion or feint to keep the British occupied. "The House this instant shakes with the Roar of Cannon," wrote Abigail Adams. On the night of March 4, Washington's army "took full possession of those heights without the loss of a single man."[23] The next morning Howe made preparations to attack but he was hindered by terrible storms. He was also impressed by the colonial fortifications. "I know not what I shall do," an impressed Howe was reported to have said, "the rebels have done more in one night than my whole army would have done in weeks."[24]

Washington, too, was pleased with the results. As a result of the colonials' preparation, "much blood was Saved, and a very important blow (to one side or the other) prevented," he wrote his brother Jack. "That this remarkable Interposition of Providence is for some wise purpose I have no doubt"; with pride the general concluded that no one "since the institution of armies" had ever commanded one under more difficult terms and that if he were to detail them "it would fill a volume."[25] Abigail Adams commented to her husband, "Our General may say with Caesar, veni, vidi, vici," (I came, I saw, I conquered).[26]

Three days later, pickets noted British activity as cannon, troops, and baggage were loaded on transports. Washington received word that if the Americans allowed a peaceful retreat the British would not torch Boston. He agreed and finally, on

March 17, the British set sail, anchoring nine miles away at Nantasket Road but still in view of the Bostonians.

Fearing disease, especially the dreaded smallpox, Washington was reluctant to enter the city. After a few days of reconnoitering the area, however, the victorious Continental Army moved into Boston. There they discovered a large supply of British goods abandoned by the retreating forces. They also found the Old South Church had been profaned: altar and pews ripped out, it had been used as a pigsty. The North Church, made famous years later by Longfellow ("one if by land, two if by sea"), fared no better; it was turned into a horse stable. The hated British driven out, Washington was proclaimed a hero.

He would have little time to bask in his glory. Still, for the moment the limelight belonged to him. He had accomplished what many considered impossible. Congress agreed to strike a gold medal in his honor, Harvard awarded him an honorary doctor of laws degree, and even the African-born poetess Phillis Wheatley honored him in verse:

> Proceed, great chief, with virtue on thy side,
> Thy ev'ry action let the goddess guide.[27]

In less than one year Washington had put in motion the process that would eventually convert his mismatched rabble into an army capable of defeating the finest military in the world.

SIX

New York

We have therefore to resolve to conquer or die.

—GEORGE WASHINGTON

WASHINGTON ARRIVED IN New York on April 12, 1776, convinced this was the next British target and the key to defending America. New York, previously the British military headquarters, contained more Tories (those whose loyalty remained with England)—perhaps two-thirds of the residents were British loyalists—than any other city. Even the royally appointed governor, William Tryon, kept a headquarters aboard a King's ship. Nonetheless, the four-thousand-pound gold-leafed lead statue of King George on horseback, located at the tip of Manhattan, had recently been vandalized.[1] Tension between rebels and loyalists was almost palpable as Washington entered the city. Open trade between civilian and British ships in the harbor, the threat of rebel desertions at the expected British arrival, and the harassment of militia recruiters in the countryside all demonstrated the strength of the Tory influence. Aware of the threat, Washington responded by forming a system of spies to keep him apprised of Tory activities.[2]

New York proper covered a square mile and contained some four thousand buildings on lower Manhattan. Because control of the city meant control of the waterways around the city, British occupation would be a disaster to the fledgling rebellion. Geographically, Manhattan would be difficult to defend, with the wide Hudson River flowing down from Albany on the west and the East River opposite. The King's Bridge in the north was the only exit from "York Island" (as it was called) on foot. New England could easily be cut off from the rest of the country if control of the Hudson fell into British hands.

Realizing the strategic nature of the city, Washington petitioned Congress for troops from Jersey "to prevent an evil, which may be almost irremediable, should It happen: I mean the landing of Troops at that place [Manhattan], or upon Long Island near it."[3] He was also aware that his own troops were not yet up to the task of defending the city. "We have nothing . . . to depend upon but the protection of a kind Providence and Unanimity among ourselves," he confided to John Adams.[4]

At the end of May, Washington traveled to Philadelphia to consult with Congress about the defense of New York. He expected an attack any day. Although peace delegates from Britain were on the way, his mood had turned to independence.

"Things have come to that pass now," he wrote his brother John, "as to convince us, that we have nothing more to expect from the justice of G: Britain . . . We expect a very bloody Summer of it at New York & Canada, as it is there I expect the grand efforts of the Enemy will be aim'd." He had neither the men nor the arms to defend the city. "However it is to be hoped that if our cause is just, as I do most religiously believe it to be, the same Providence which has in many Instances appeard for us, will still go on to afford its aid."[5]

On a personal note, he added that Martha, who had joined him in mid-April, had recently been inoculated for smallpox. This procedure consisted of giving the patient a mild case of the disease and quarantining her for two or three weeks. She was nearing the end of this period and "has very few Pustules." The pox and other diseases would become more deadly than enemy fire, and within two years Washington ordered all troops to be inoculated. The scars on his nose attested to the fact that Washington had contracted a mild case of the pox while a youth in Barbados, which provided his own immunity.[6]

Soon after his return from Philadelphia, Washington's intelligence service uncovered a plot that originated in the governor's office and also involved the mayor. They intended to blow up American powder magazines, fire the city, and even assassinate Washington. Immediately, twenty conspirators were arrested, including two of Washington's bodyguards, one of whom, Thomas Hickey, was convicted and publicly hanged. Washington ordered the spectacle, witnessed by an immense cheering crowd, as an example to all. General orders for the following day included the advice for soldiers to "avoid lewd Women, who, by the dying Confession of this poor Criminal first led him into the practices which ended in an untimely and ignominious Death."[7]

This plot inflamed the passions of the patriots who swarmed into the streets to punish any loyalist they could find. Several were grabbed, beaten, tarred and feathered, or burned with candle wax. Tarring and feathering, previously used against tax collectors in Boston, was a crowd favorite. The victim was stripped as hot tar was liberally applied from the head down. The unfortunate Tory was then rolled in chicken feathers. If the mob was particularly incensed, they could ride the man out of town on a rail. This was done by forcing the victim to straddle a split rail—which was sharpened to inflict maximum discomfort—while two men pulled down on his legs. He was then "ridden" out of town to the cheers of the taunting crowd. Two or three months passed before the tar-stained, blistered skin grew back.

On April 29, Washington made one of his best decisions of the war: he selected Brigadier Nathanael Greene, at thirty-two the youngest brigadier appointed, to command the forces on Long Island. Greene was a former Quaker who had been asked to leave his spiritual fellowship because he rejected pacifism. He had initially enlisted as a private in the Rhode Island brigade but was soon selected to lead the unit. His civilian life had prepared him for command, as he had long overseen more than two hundred men at his family's foundry. It helped that he was physically impressive and his spit-and-polish approach to his troops endeared him to Washington. Thanks largely to Greene's gifts, the unit he commanded at Boston was head and shoulders above the rest, both in discipline and neatness. It was Greene who wisely and humanely counseled Congress that if they would "fix a certain support upon every Officer and Soldier that got maim'd in the service or upon the families of those that were kild, enlistments would improve."[8]

During the months of May and June, the Continental Army prepared for the expected attack. The challenges were great. When would Howe arrive? How many troops would he have? Most importantly, where would he come ashore? Although Knox had 121 cannon, it was not enough given the area to be covered. To prevent the British fleet from going up the Hudson River to Albany, head engineer Colonel Rufus Putnam erected a defensive site utilizing many of the cannon. This battery came to be known as Fort Washington and was built on the highest point of Manhattan, 230 feet above the river. Coupled with Fort Lee, which was constructed on the New Jersey side of the river, Knox had a commanding field of fire on any advancing ships.[9]

To defend Brooklyn, the key to protecting Long Island, Greene also had men digging. Soldiers dug trenches miles long that connected five small forts. Between the trenches, *chevaux-de-frise* were placed. These portable obstacles, which consisted of logs adorned with iron spikes for quills and resembled porcupines, were designed to stop cavalry and slow down charging troops. Larger *chevaux-de-frise* strung along the surface of the river could slow or stop ships. Mechanical measures such as these evened the scales of battle. Washington realized he had to split his inexperienced forces, normally not a sound military decision but—without knowing Howe's exact plans—a necessary one.

By July 2, Washington had some of the answers to his questions. Lord Richard Howe, or "Black Dick" as he was known due to his swarthy complexion, had anchored 130 ships in the Lower Bay. The general orders for July 2, 1776, warned of the impending attack. Exhibit a "great coolness in time of action," Washington commanded his officers. Soldiers were exhorted to maintain "a strict attention and obedience, with a becoming firmness and spirit."[10] All were to remain within the sound of the drum call ready for action at a moment's notice. Rain appeared imminent, so particular care was to be taken to keep their powder dry. The general continued,

> The time is now near at hand which must probably determine, whether Americans are to be Freemen, or Slaves; whether they are to have any property they can call their own; whether their Houses, Farms, are to be pillaged and destroyed, and they consigned to a State of Wretchedness from which no human efforts will ever deliver them . . . The fate of unborn Millions will now depend, under God, on the Courage and Conduct of this army . . . We have therefore to resolve to conquer or die . . . Let us therefore rely upon the goodness of the Cause, and the aid of the supreme Being, in whose hands Victory is to animate and encourage us to great and noble Actions—The Eyes of all our Countrymen are now upon us . . . [11]

On the same day in Philadelphia, Congress approved the Declaration of Independence. "Altho it is not possible to foresee the Consequences of Human Actions," Hancock wrote

Washington, "yet it is nevertheless a Duty we owe ourselves and Posterity . . . to decide in the best Manner we are able, and to leave the Event to that Being who controuls both Causes and Events to bring about his own Determinations." With his letter, he included a copy of the document and ordered him to make the contents known "in the Way you shall think most proper."[12] On July 9, one of Washington's aides read the declaration to a gathered crowd in New York.

Washington's response to the declaration was neutral yet hopeful. "I perceive that Congress have been employed in deliberating on measures of the most Interesting nature," he wrote Hancock, "but yet It behoves us to adopt such, as under the smiles of a Gracious & All kind Providence will be most likely to promote our happiness . . . and will secure us that freedom and those privileges which have been and are refused us, contrary to the voice of nature and the British Constitution."[13]

The general orders for July 9 expressed the general's hope that the declaration by Congress would "serve as a fresh incentive to every officer, and soldier, to act with Fidelity and Courage, as knowing that now the peace and safety of his Country depends (under God) solely on the success of our arms." Congress also provided for a chaplain, "with the pay of Thirty-three Dollars and one third a month" to be recruited for each regiment. Chaplains were to be "persons of good Character and exemplary lives." Furthermore, commanders were to see that they received all due respect and all soldiers were required to attend religious services. "The blessing and protection of Heaven are at all times necessary but especially so in times of public distress and danger—The

General hopes and trusts that every officer, and man, will endeavor so to live, and act, as becomes a Christian Soldier, defending the dearest Rights and Liberties of his country," the orders concluded.[14]

That evening rowdy soldiers celebrated the news of the declaration by tearing down the statue of King George. Cutting off the monarch's head, they stole the gold leaf and eventually melted down the lead for bullets to be used against the king's redcoats. The next day Washington condemned this action, as it had the "appearance of riot and want of order," and "in future these things shall be avoided by the Soldiery." Washington was incensed but soon had greater problems than a few rowdy soldiers.[15]

Nearly a week later the general received a letter from Admiral Howe, asking to meet and discuss the "King's benevolent intentions" that could lead to "preventing the further Effusion of Blood, and become productive of Peace and lasting Union between Great Britain and America."[16] Howe, perhaps motivated by self-interest since he received special pay as the King's peace commissioner, had political aspirations. He wrote letters to colonial governors and Ben Franklin and asked for their aid in bringing about a peaceful solution. He dangled the carrot of future favor before them if they assisted him. The admiral also scattered pamphlets offering pardons for any soldier who returned to civilian life.

When British Lieutenant Philip Brown from the admiral's flagship *Eagle* attempted to deliver the letter, he discovered the colonials were acquainted with the symbolism accompanying protocol. In the late eighteenth century, formality both in dress and discourse was expected. Titles were important and those who had them expected to be addressed by them. Washington sent his trusted colonels Joseph Reed and Henry Knox in a whaleboat to receive Howe's letter. When Brown received the pair aboard his barge, he doffed his hat, bowed, and stated, "I have a letter, sir, from Lord Howe to Mr. Washington." Wanting to send Howe a message of how things had changed in the world, Reed responded, "Sir, we have no person in the army with that address." Brown tried to press the letter on Reed, but Reed refused to accept or even touch it. As Brown left he inquired as to how Washington wished to be addressed, to which Reed responded, "You are sensible, sir, of the rank of General Washington in our army? All the world knows who General Washington is since the transactions of last summer."[17]

Washington could not receive the letter without his official title for two reasons. First, formality mattered. Second, Washington wanted to make the point he was no longer simply a private citizen capable of individual negotiation with the Crown, but was representative of and under the authority of Congress. Upon hearing of this transaction, Congress "highly" approved.[18]

On July 20, Howe's adjutant, Lieutenant Colonel James Patterson, arrived with the letter at 1 Broad Street, the address of Washington's mansion. Attempting to soothe over Washington's feelings by reminding him that only last summer he [Washington] had written a letter to General Howe, addressing him as "the Hon. William Howe, Esqe," Patterson placed the letter on the table. This time it had the same address,

"George Washington, Esq." but added "&c.&c.&c." [etc. etc. etc.]. Washington declined the letter once again, stating that "a letter directed to a person in publick Character should have some Description or Indication of it otherwise it would appear a mere Letter." Although the "&c.&c.&c. implied every thing & they also implied any thing," Patterson tried one more approach. In a conversation with Washington, he asserted the king had appointed the Howes to reach a peace agreement and had invested in them "great powers." Washington responded they were vested only with power to grant pardons to rebels. "Those who had committed no Fault wanted no Pardon," answered Washington. Patterson left with the unopened letter.[19]

In their conversation, Washington had also protested the treatment of captured Americans in Boston. The lack of care for colonial POWs, many of whom were placed in the bowels of old warships that had little light and who were given poor food and rancid water, would be a constant source of concern and protest by Washington throughout the war. Patterson argued they were treated well. Upon hearing of the interchange between Washington and Patterson, Lord Howe expressed his feeling that chances of peace were now over. The solution would have to be a military one; thus British forces continued on the move.

On August 1, American observers noted a fleet of some forty-five ships off Sandy Hook. The badly battered vessels, commanded by General Henry Clinton with his second in command, Lord Charles Cornwallis, had just arrived from Charles Town. The good news was that the South Carolina city, under the command of Charles Lee, had survived their attack. The bad news was that Howe now had an additional three thousand troops with which to attack New York.

Other bad news reached Washington's ears. His troops in Canada had been routed and were holed up in Fort Ticonderoga. More than British bullets, disease, and smallpox in particular took its toll on the poorly supplied and hungry soldiers. Medicine was in its infancy and a "good" surgeon was one who could amputate quickly and thereby prevent shock from killing the patient. Men died and died horribly, as was happening at Fort Ticonderoga.

In a congratulatory letter to Lee for his success in South Carolina, Washington confided, "At present the Enemy can bring more men to a point than we can . . . and when re-inforced by the Hessians will outnumber Us." Washington believed the enemy had twenty-five thousand troops to his less than twenty thousand. His garrison was "very sickly" and posted thinly all over the area. The exact point of attack was still only a guess.[20]

Over the next few weeks the combined might of the British forces grew. With the arrival on August 12 of another hundred ships, the force now facing the Americans was the largest expeditionary action of the eighteenth century—over four hundred ships. Of them, seventy-three were warships, and eight of these were ships of the line carrying at least fifty guns. The ships alone could bring twelve hundred cannon to bear upon the enemy. British ships were designated by the number of cannon they carried. First-rate ships, such as Admiral Nelson's *Victory*, carried at least one hundred guns, divided between the two sides with three gun decks. The crew alone on one of these leviathans numbered over eight hundred officers and men. Accordingly, a force of thirty-four thousand trained foot soldiers and cavalry troops now faced the Continental Army. This force was larger than any American city of the day, even Philadelphia. Against such a juggernaut, Washington could muster a poorly trained, sadly equipped, thinly scattered force of only twenty-three thousand, many of whom were unfit for duty due to sickness. The battle for New York and the predicted "very bloody Summer" was about to begin.

SEVEN

Long Island

Good god have I got such troops as those?

—GEORGE WASHINGTON

ON THE EVENING of August 21, 1776, a violent storm hit New York. Thunder crashed "louder than a thousand cannon discharged at once." Rain fell in torrents and lightning fell like "fire to the earth." Three American officers were hit by lightning, leaving "the points of their swords melted off, and the coin melted in their pockets."[1] A witness said their bodies looked as "if they had been roasted, so black and crisped was the skin." Ten others were killed by one flash of lightning. Major Benedict believed this event had a "hidden meaning, some secret purpose, when the bolt is launched by an invisible arm, and from the mysterious depth of space." His answer was that perhaps "the vast amount of arms collected in and about the city" had somehow created an attraction that "drew from it such a fearful amount of electricity."[2]

August 22 dawned blue and clear. For three hours four hundred British transport ships disgorged nearly fifteen thousand troops, and the Americans viewed the blue coats and yellow pants of the hated Hessians for the first time. These mercenaries, hired mostly from the German state of Hesse, were well-trained and well-equipped. Many Americans cried foul at the hiring of foreigners to fight in what they considered a family feud. In addition to the Hessians and redcoats, the Americans also saw kilted Scottish troops undoubtedly blowing their bagpipes, a sound designed to instill fear in the enemy. Most surprising was the sight of black slaves promised freedom to enlist with the British. Initially, Washington forbade the enlistment of even free blacks. Lord Dunmore, however, had forced him to change his mind. In November 1775, while Royal Governor of Virginia, Dunmore created his "Ethiopian Regiment." While relatively few in number, they had an impact on colonial thinking and Washington would reluctantly come to understand not only the necessity of recruiting blacks but also their skill.[3]

The newly appointed Major General Nathanael Greene was responsible for the defense of Long Island. He was the one man who knew the topography well. Unfortunately, he had fallen ill with a "putrid and bilious fever" ten days previously.[4] Washington chose Brigadier General John Sullivan as replacement. "He is active, spirited, and zealously attach'd to the Cause," Washington wrote, with "a little tincture of vanity, and in an over desire of being popular, which now and then leads him into some embarrassments." Overall, however, Sullivan only lacked what all colonial leaders lacked—experience.[5]

Furious at what he saw was a slight to his rank and position, the fifty-eight-year-old Major General Israel Putnam complained. Making a major blunder, Washington succumbed to pressure and replaced Sullivan after only four days in command. The new commander for the crucial defense of Long Island knew nothing of the terrain or troop disposition. Putnam's inexperience, coupled with Washington's failure to personally reconnoiter the topography, were enough to lead to sure defeat.

The sight of the vast forces arrayed against them caused many Americans to flee and further weaken an already anemic defense. On August 23, Washington utilized his general orders to exhort the faltering resolve of his militia.

> The Enemy has now landed on Long Island, and the hour is fast approaching, on which the Honor and Success of this army, and the safety of our bleeding Country depend. Remember officers and Soldiers, that you are Freemen, fighting for the blessings of Liberty—that slavery will be your portion, and that of your posterity, if you do not acquit yourselves like men . . . Be cool but determined; do not fire at a distance, but wait for orders from your officers—It is the General's express orders that if any man attempt to skulk, lay down, or retreat without Orders he be instantly shot down as an example.[6]

Apparently the men did not heed the orders. Old Put's men were pillaging and burning property, wasting ammunition by randomly shooting, and acting in an "unsoldierlike and undisciplined" manner. "The distinction between a well regulated army, & a mob, is the good order & discipline of the first," the general scolded Putnam, "& the licentious & disorderly behavior of the latter."[7] Skirmishing was okay providing it was under the authority of either an officer or noncommissioned officer.

The British landed at Gravesend on the south side of Long Island about ten miles from the American position. It was relatively flat and level without any significant tree cover until about three miles from the American lines at Brooklyn Heights. There the terrain changed to "woods and broken ground." To reach the Heights the British had to choose one of four passes. Reconnoitering the area, Clinton discovered that Jamaica Pass, the left flank of the Americans, was unguarded. Washington ordered Putnam to guard Guana Pass on his right flank with "your best men," who should "at all hazards prevent the enemy's passing the wood; & approaching your works." There Putnam placed three thousand troops under the command of the British-born lawyer William Alexander, who had assumed the title Lord Stirling.[8]

The attack began well after dark on August 26. Howe's tactics were simple. Feint to the Guana Pass side, force Putnam to commit his reserves, then attack through Jamaica Pass and flank the Americans. These tactics worked brilliantly. General James Grant led his forces up the road to Guana; the Hessians, commanded by General Philip von Heister, charged the center; and Howe, Clinton, and Cornwallis brought ten thousand troops and twenty-eight cannon through the unguarded pass. The flanking maneuver caught the Americans off guard and, coupled with the darkness, caused widespread panic. At daybreak both Stirling and Sullivan discovered the British at their rear—between them and the safety of Brooklyn Heights.

The British controlled the main thoroughfares so the Americans had to straggle back through woods and swampy ground. During the retreat, pitched battles among small groups of soldiers took place all along the line. As the discipline and fire of the Hessians took its toll, many of the fleeing troops were bayoneted, while others surrendered. Sullivan himself was captured along with an American flag. Although the Delaware and Maryland contingents along the left flank fought well, they, too, had to retreat either by wading through Gowanus Creek or by diving into the ocean and swimming to safety. Fifteen-year-old Joseph Plumb Martin had joined the army at New York, wanting to "snuff a little gunpowder." In his memoirs, published in 1830, he described the escaping Marylanders as "looking like water rats," as they came out of the mud and water.[9]

A little after noon, the British smashed through the defenses and reached the outskirts of Brooklyn Heights. With twenty thousand disciplined and eager troops facing less than five thousand disorganized Americans, Clinton urged Howe to finish the job. Either luck or Washington's Providence intervened: Howe ordered the attack to cease. Why? Perhaps he wanted to prevent further bloodshed. Perhaps his intent was to give his troops a rest. Or maybe it was just his cautious nature—where could the Americans go? Their back was up against the East River. His brother, the admiral, controlled the passage across the water to Manhattan. Time was on his side—or so he thought.

The day after the Battle of Long Island Washington reviewed his options. The British had captured one thousand men, including generals Stirling and Sullivan. The "butcher's bill" was three hundred dead and many more wounded. His frightened, sick, tired, hungry troops tried to find shelter from a cold rain; tents were scarce. "In the latter part of the afternoon there fell a heavy shower of rain," reported Martin, "which wet us all to the skin and much damaged our ammunition." The bread was "hard enough to break the teeth of a rat."[10] Only weather and wind prevented Lord Howe from closing off the way of escape. Although seemingly trapped, Washington was prepared to fight, not retreat, as reinforcements arrived with Brigadier General Thomas Mifflin and his Pennsylvania Brigade. Mifflin had political experience; he was a member of Congress in 1774. As an aide-de-camp to Washington and a former quartermaster general, he knew the military. Among the replacements was a man who became one of Washington's ablest and most trusted officers—Colonel John Glover.

Along with Colonel Israel Hutchinson, Glover commanded a unit of some of the most disciplined and hardened men in America. Fishermen from the coastal Massachusetts cities of Salem, Marblehead, Lynn, and Danvers, and used to working aboard ship under extreme weather and sea conditions, these men understood the taking and obeying of orders. These "amphibious units" were men who "dressed in white caps, short blue coats, and canvas breeches waterproofed with tar." Their professionalism and calm attitude helped rally the morale of the beaten men. Pennsylvania Captain Alexander Graydon was impressed with most of Glover's men, but noted, "even in this regiment there were a number of negroes, which . . . had a disagreeable, degrading effect."[11]

After consultation with his officers, the commander in chief decided discretion was the better part of valor. His army was to retreat from Long Island as soon as possible. British sappers had extended their trenches ever closer to the weakened Americans and attack seemed imminent. Retreat across the East River, however, meant the army must show its back to the advancing redcoats while at the same time protect themselves from British ships. The ten flatboats available to transport ninety-five hundred men and all their weapons, cannon, and supplies across the nearly mile-wide river looked inadequate. Messengers searched the coastline for anything that would float. To prevent panic among the men and information leaking to Howe, Washington confided his plan to only his closest aides. Again luck or Providence intervened. Rain persisted and on August 29 a thick fog and mist descended.

At eight o'clock, with darkness falling, Glover's fishermen began the daunting mission of ferrying men and equipment across the river. "At this time a very dense fog began to rise, and it seemed to settle in a peculiar manner over both encampments," wrote Benjamin Tallmadge, future manager of Washington's secret service. He later recalled "this peculiar providential occurrence perfectly well; and so very dense was the atmosphere that I could scarcely discern a man at six yards' distance."[12] At least one Marblehead mariner made the two-mile trip eleven times. Wrapping oars in cloth to prevent any sound from carrying across the water, the oarsmen fought not only the lack of visibility but also currents and wind. The fog began to clear off about seven a.m., after all Americans had made their escape.

As a ruse, Washington ordered campfires to burn brightly as the units departed one by one. "We were strictly enjoined not to talk, or even cough," noted Martin, as they moved to the transports. About ten hours later, after the army had successfully made its escape, the British attacked and overran the now deserted Brooklyn Heights. Continental losses amounted to three troops, who had remained to loot, and several cannon lodged in the mud. Washington, the last to cross, and his ragged army were spared to fight another day.[13]

The crossing did not mean the army was safe. New York lay at the bottom of a peninsula. Howe merely had to land further north, cross Manhattan, and they were trapped. No one knew this better than Washington. "Our situation is truly distressing," he informed Congress on September 2. "The check our Detachment sustained on the 27th Ulto ["last month" or August] has dispirited a too great proportion of our Troops and filled their mind with apprehension and despair." In his description of the battle, he singled out the militia for special criticism. "The Militia, instead of calling forth their utmost efforts to a brave & manly opposition . . . are dismayed, Intractable, and Impatient to return. Great numbers of them have gone off . . . almost by whole Regiments—by half Ones & by Companies at a time." An attitude of despair filled the camp as many demonstrated a "refusal of almost every kind of restraint & Government." He needed professional troops.[14]

Americans had long feared a professional standing army. The redcoat occupation of Boston still stuck in their minds. Many immigrants had escaped persecution imposed by professional soldiers. Most believed that a civilian militia, raised up to fight for their homes when threatened by an immediate enemy, would better protect their liberties. The minutemen, private citizens who could quickly grab their weapons ready to oppose any immediate threat, constituted their ideal. Many in Congress were suspicious when Washington proposed a professional standing regular army. "I am persuaded and fully convinced, as I am of any One fact that has happened," he proposed, "that our Liberties must of necessity be greatly hazarded, If not entirely lost If their defence is left to any but a permanent, standing Army I mean One to exist during the War."[15] Free men, quickly called and untrained, could not readily submit to the rigid discipline necessary to defend against well-trained, well-equipped forces.

Recognizing that the situation in lower Manhattan was untenable, he decided to march north. "The City and Suburbs should be burnt," recommended Greene, thus leaving no shelter or supplies to the enemy. Although Washington agreed, Congress expressly ordered him not to do so. He could flee north, but not burn the city. Before leaving, he took whatever remained of value, including the Anglican Church bells. Used to warn of emergencies, such as fire, as well as call the faithful to prayer, they were later melted into cannon or shot. The poorly organized retreat, made worse by lax discipline and poor attitudes among the militia, commenced on September 13, with the goal of getting off the island of Manhattan and out of a possible trap.[16]

The Howe brothers also realized the American predicament and set out to exploit it. The day of the American retreat, Admiral Howe sent warships and transports loaded with four thousand troops up the East River to land at Kip's Bay. On the fifteenth, under a fierce covering bombardment by the British warships, they came ashore over the course of an hour and were joined by nine thousand additional troops in the afternoon. Private Martin recorded that the enemy troops were so many and so tightly packed "they appeared like a large clover field in full bloom."[17] Trained to march side by side, bayonets extended and to the beat of a marshal drum, the redcoats were one of the most feared armies in the world. They were disciplined not to flinch if the man on either side of them went down and wore stiff stocks around their necks that forced them to look straight ahead. They were an impressive sight and had broken many armies around the world.

Washington, having taken up a position four miles to the north on Harlem Heights, heard the roar of the cannon and observed the enemy coming ashore. Racing south he passed many militia fleeing the opposite direction. Instinctively he recognized the advantage of taking the high ground at a place now known as Murray Hill. Urging his horse up the hill, he met brigadier generals Holden Parsons and John Fellows arriving with their eight regiments. Coming up the other side of the hill was the British regular army. The sight of the British regulars, accompanied by the Hessians, made many military break ranks and run.

Seeing his troops again flee in panic, Washington lost his usual control. "I used every means in my power to rally and get them into some order," he complained later to Hancock, "but my attempts were fruitless and ineffectual, and on the appearance of a small party of the Enemy, not more than Sixty or Seventy . . . they ran away in the greatest confusion, without firing a Single Shot."[18] Washington "struck several officers in their flight, three times dashed his hatt on the ground, and at last exclaimed 'Good god have I got such troops as those?'" commented Colonel George Weedon, a former colleague of the General's in Virginia.[19]

The Marylander Colonel Smallwood, also appalled at the lack of courage, observed that the fleeing men "were caned and whipped by the Generals Washington, Putnam, and Mifflin, but even this indignity had no weight, they could not be brought to stand one shot."[20] So distracted was Washington that at one point he was only eighty yards from the enemy and had to be forced to fall back. The British captured most of the 350 or so men, as well as baggage, cannons, and supplies—something the Continental Army could not afford to lose. If Howe had followed up this victory and continued to cross the width of Manhattan, he might easily have captured nearly a quarter of all American troops yet again he paused.

"In confidence I tell you that I never was in such an unhappy, divided state since I was born," wrote a disconsolate Washington to his cousin Lund Washington. The militia officers were not "except in a few instances, worth the bread they eat." The men were "plundering and marauding," and were more threat to the local farmers and residents than to the enemy. "In short, such is my situation that if I were to wish the bitterest curse to an enemy on this side of the grave, I should put him in my stead with my feelings; and yet I do not know what plan of conduct to pursue."

He expressed his desire to resign and let another command. Duty and honor prevented him, however, and he resolved, "not to be forced from this ground while I have life."[21]

With keen insight into human nature, Washington recognized that men will fight only so long out of patriotism before self-interest takes over. "When Men are irritated, & the Passions inflamed, they fly hastily and chearfully to Arms," he wrote Congress, "but after the first emotions are over, to expect . . . that they are influenced by any other principles than those of Interest, is to look for what never did, & I fear never will happen." Congress deluded itself if it believed otherwise. In order to enlist and keep officers, and by this he meant gentlemen, "They ought to have such allowances as will enable them to live like, and support the Characters of Gentlemen; and not be driven by a scanty pittance to the low & dirty arts which many of them practices." The general concluded this long letter by reaffirming that the problems associated with a standing army pale in comparison to not having one as the consequence "is certain and inevitable Ruin."[22]

While Washington was at Harlem Heights laying the groundwork for a professional army, thirty-five hundred troops under the command of colonels Gold Silliman and Henry Knox remained in Manhattan and would soon be cut off from retreat. The stranded American militia was saved only due to the growing rift between the conservative strategy of British General Howe and that of his second in command, Henry Clinton. Had Howe heeded Clinton's advice and immediately sealed the escape route, he might have succeeded in capturing the rebels. At four o'clock on a blistering hot afternoon, Major Aaron Burr led the two-mile-long column on a forced march of twelve miles up the Bloomingdale Road on the west side of the island. At the same time the British advance force marched down the east side of Manhattan arriving in the city at five o'clock, again just missing the chance to deliver a knockout blow.

Baron Von Steuben training troops at Valley Forge.

Major Gen. Henry Knox

The Hon[ora]ble S[i]r William Howe, Knight of the
Bath and Commander in Chief and Commander of his
Magesty's forces in America (1778).

Infantry of the Continental Army 1779–1783.

EIGHT

Harlem Heights and White Plains

It was the most hellish scene I ever beheld.

—CHARLES WILSON PEALE, ARTIST

ON SEPTEMBER 16, Washington was finally in a geographically tenable position. From the heights of Harlem he surveyed the terrain and troop movement below. Directly to his south was a narrow valley named the Hollow Way, easily covered by artillery fire. To the west lay the Harlem Plains and to his east the rocky terrain dropped off to the Hudson. Desperate to know what the enemy was up to, Washington sent out scouting parties to gather intelligence. One of these units was Colonel Knowlton's Connecticut Ranger corps. The thirty-seven-year-old Knowlton had earned a reputation of being a "soldier's soldier" at the battle of Bunker Hill. Several days earlier a captain from his unit, Nathan Hale, had been sent undercover to spy out the activity in Manhattan.

General Howe was also comfortably situated, with his headquarters at the splendid estate of Mount Pleasant overlooking the East River in Manhattan. His northernmost troops were encamped just south of the Hollow Way out of sight. Just before sunup Knowlton's scouting party came upon the outermost British pickets. What followed was the Battle of Harlem Heights.

With bugles blaring, the British fired upon the Rangers, who in turn began a slow retreat. Joseph Reed, Washington's adjutant, reported to Washington that when the two sides met, the British bugles began playing the call used to summon fox hunters to the chase "in a most insulting manner." Tired of retreating and insulted by the tune, the former fox-hunting gentleman displayed the leadership and bravery that made him famous. He ordered reinforcements to attack.[1]

Washington tried to lure the British troops into the Hollow Way where his artillery could do its work. At the same time he ordered troops to flank the oncoming redcoats. The plan almost worked, but an impatient officer fired and warned the British before the encircling troops had time to get into position. Still the fighting was fierce. The hottest part of the battle lasted about an hour and took place in a buckwheat field encompassed by a rail fence. "I myself counted nineteen ball-holes through a single rail of the fence," reported Martin. As the exhausted and starving men—who had not eaten in forty-eight hours—rested, one man complained of hunger. An officer pulled out an ear of Indian corn, "burnt as black as coal," handed it to him with the admonition "eat this and learn to be a soldier." Both sides incurred about 150 casualties but the battle boosted the morale of the bedraggled and disillusioned Americans. Knowlton's Rangers had fought well and stood up to the famed Scottish Black Watch Highlanders and Hessian *Jaegers* and forced them to retreat. Unfortunately, Knowlton was killed during the fight.[2]

On September 21, a mysterious fire erupted in New York, destroying a thousand buildings—nearly one quarter of the city. Each side blamed the other for setting it: Howe blamed Washington, who had earlier removed the church bells used to warn the citizenry; the Tories blamed the rebels for destroying their property; and the rebels claimed the Tories were responsible. The Hessians used it as an opportunity to loot.[3]

In addition to producing property damage and loss of life, this incident precipitated two significant events. First, the American spy Nathan Hale was captured with incriminating evidence on his person. Although Hale was an officer, he was not in uniform and was behind enemy lines. This meant he would hang. "He behaved with great composure and resolution," wrote the British eyewitness Captain Frederick MacKenzie. Hale's final words were probably not "I only regret I have but one life to lose for my country" but he did appear "to be at all times prepared to meet death in whatever shape it might appear," according to MacKenzie.[4]

The second, more subtle event was the beginning of a policy that slowly turned the neutral portion of the American civilian population against the British war effort. At this time the Howe brothers commanded over half of the entire worldwide British military. The supply line for this enormous force was three thousand miles long across a treacherous and unpredictable sea. General Howe began confiscating desperately needed housing, medical facilities, and supplies for his men. He also clamped down on public dissidence and declared martial law. Although New Yorkers initially accepted these policies because they were desperate to have order in the city, they soon realized they had lost all personal liberties. To be successful, an army of occupation must have the support of the local civilian population in order to "live off the land." The British, though, alienated not only the formerly neutral citizenry but also some of the Tory population, as well. This would prove disastrous.

Howe rested his troops until Friday, October 11, 1776, when he decided once again to attack Washington and drive the Continental Army from New York. Hoping to trap Washington at Harlem, the British navy sailed up the East River. Hidden by a dense fog they passed through the treacherous currents of Hell Gate and the next day unloaded four thousand troops at Throg's Neck, a marshy island at high tide. But the difficult terrain, made more treacherous by the marksmanship of thirty Pennsylvanian long rifles, soon halted the British.

Washington realized that remaining in Harlem was not an option. It was only a matter of time before Howe encircled him. Conferring with his council of generals, he decided to retreat, leaving behind twelve hundred isolated troops at Fort Washington to protect the Hudson. On the seventeenth he moved his army twenty miles north across the King's Bridge and into the town of White Plains. There he established a three-mile-long front line. He placed only a few hundred men on the high ground—Chatterton Hill. Howe's troops followed, landing three miles north of Throg's Neck at Pell's Point, and quickly moved inland. He might have caught up with the fleeing Americans, but Colonel Glover again saved the day for his general.

Just before daybreak, October 18, Glover, left as a rear guard, spotted "upwards of 200 sail all manned." With spirit and determination he and his 750 men hid behind stone walls and began firing. His men inflicted heavy casualties and suffered but eight dead and thirteen wounded. Stung by the resistance, Howe was stalled for three days. "Oh! The anxiety of mind I was in then for the fate of the day," Glover later lamented. "I would have given a thousand worlds to have had General Lee, or some experienced officer present to direct, or at least approve what I had done."[5] On the twenty-first Howe occupied New Rochelle and two days later received four thousand Hessian reinforcements. The time had come to lure Washington into a pitched battle and end this war.

Howe had thirteen thousand troops, mainly German, to attack Chatterton Hill. One of the Hessian brigades was led by Colonel Johann Gottlieb Rall. His disciplined troops, supported by British artillery, marched up the hill with their bayonets gleaming in the sun. Although the Continentals made a good show of it, they were no match for the oncoming British and Germans, who, despite having about 276 casualties, won the day. Again forced to withdraw, Washington took refuge across the Bronx River in a good position on high ground. Howe chose not to attack and decided he could do more damage by returning to Manhattan and removing the final American presence at Fort Washington.

It is difficult to explain Washington's lack of decisiveness in the months that followed. Perhaps it was inexperience with a constantly shifting front. Or perhaps he was weary of constantly retreating, or felt constrained by Congressional direction. When commissioned as commander in chief in 1775, Congress stipulated decisions were only to be made, after "advising with your counsel of war." This counsel, comprised of senior generals, often disagreed, and frustrated the aggressive Washington. Although he always submitted to civilian authority, experience would soon force him to rely more on his own judgment than that of counsel. Unfortunately, the experience gained by senior officers often comes at the expense of those under them.

Fort Washington and Fort Lee had been constructed to prevent British ships from moving up the Hudson River. In theory, the *chevaux-de-frise* and sunken hulls of old ships placed in the river outside the forts were to slow down vessels and allow the cannon from the forts to blow them to bits. Unfortunately, this was not working. "The late passage of the 3 Vessells up the North [Hudson] River," Washington confided to Greene on November 8, "is so plain a Proof of the inefficacy of all the Obstructions we have thrown into it, that I cannot but think, it will fully justify a Change in the Disposition which has been made." Although he recommended abandoning the fort, since there was little value in holding an ineffective position surrounded by the enemy, Washington deferred to Greene, "But as you are on the Spot,

[I] leave it to you to give such Orders as to evacuating Mount Washington as you judge best."[6]

In addition to Greene, General Putnam and the post commander, Colonel Robert Magaw, also believed they could hold the fort. Washington's confidence in others proved to be a mistake. On November 15, Magaw received a messenger from the British who had, unbeknownst to the Americans, landed at Spuyten Duyvil Creek just north of the fort. Either surrender the post within two hours or all would be put to the sword, the message read. "We are determined to defend the post or die," Magaw blustered to the British request.[7]

At dawn Howe launched thirteen thousand men, about four times the size of the American garrison. British soldiers attacked from the river and Hessians charged on two other sides. Although fighting bravely and inflicting many casualties, especially upon the Hessians, the troops could not hold the outer perimeters. They were forced back behind the walls of the fort, a small indefensible area without a source of water. By four p.m., twenty-eight hundred soldiers—along with cannon, ammunition, and small arms—were in the hands of the British.

The helpless Washington looked on from across the Hudson in Fort Lee as his troops fought, died, and surrendered. He nearly wept with frustration at the savageness of the Hessians who, angered at seeing so many of their comrades fall, beat, kicked, and even bayoneted to death several of the prisoners until restrained by the British. As Washington watched the surrender he must have been thinking that in a few weeks enlistments would run out on about two thousand more of his troops; the entire army's enlistments ended one month later on December 31.

Washington now sunk into one of the darkest periods of his life and had to dig deep within himself to continue. "This is a most unfortunate affair," he sadly wrote his brother John on November 19, "and has given me great Mortification as we have lost not only two thousand Men . . . but a good deal of Artillery, & some of the best Arms we had." Congress dithered, bickered, and refused to act on his recommendation for a professional army and chances to win the war were dwindling. "I am wearied almost to death with the retrograde Motions of things, and I solemnly protest that a pecuniary reward of 20,000 [pounds] a year would not induce me to undergo what I do."[8] Yet persist he did throughout the coming winter.

To compound his problems he discovered his subordinates were losing faith in him. Lee, the experienced former British officer commanding some of the best continental units, was at North Castle, New York, operating somewhat independently. The self-assured Lee, who was ever working to replace Washington as commander in chief, openly challenged him. He questioned Washington's allowing Greene to make the decision to defend Fort Washington. "Oh General," he complained, "why woud you be over-perswaded by Men of inferior judgment to your own?"[9] Washington's secretary, Joseph Reed, was also disappointed in his commander, and encouraged Lee. "You have a Decision, a Quality often wanted in Minds otherwise valuable . . . Oh! General—an indecisive Mind is one of the greatest Misfortunes that can befall an Army—how often have I lamented it this Campaign."[10] Lee answered Reed, "[I] lament with you that fatal indecision of mind which in war is a much greater disqualification than stupidity or even want of personal courage."[11]

By chance Washington intercepted and read the letter to Reed. Stunned but not angry, he forwarded the letter to Reed without reproach. Nearly six months would pass before Reed tried to explain his actions. Reed had not expected his original letter to provoke such a reaction from Lee. Problems with Lee, however, were just beginning.

On the British side, Howe placed General Charles Cornwallis, a highborn aristocrat and career soldier, in charge of the expedition to chase and capture Washington. Cornwallis, like both Howe brothers, was a Whig and desired to make peace with the Americans. Much to the frustration of his subordinates, he often tried to avoid direct and costly encounters with the rebels. Time and again he allowed Washington's ragged army to escape when a decisive blow could have been struck. On the other side of the British command was Henry Clinton, a royalist Tory. He wanted to strike hard and fast and quickly capture or kill all rebel forces. Since Howe agreed with Cornwallis, he placed Cornwallis in charge of forcing the Americans out of eastern New Jersey. He wanted it done quickly but with minimal casualties, before winter brought an end to the campaign season. Howe sent Clinton off to take Rhode Island.[12]

On November 20, Howe ordered Cornwallis to capture Fort Lee. As it had no tactical significance, Washington ordered the fort evacuated. Forced to flee in haste, the two-thousand–man garrison lost more precious equipment. Although within sight of the fleeing Americans, Cornwallis ordered Captain Johann Ewald's company of Hessian *Jaegers* to halt pursuit. Questioning the order, Ewald received the same answer. "Now I perceived what was afoot," he reflected in his diary, "We wanted to spare the King's subjects and hoped to terminate the war amicably, in which assumption I was strengthened the next day by several British officers." This was neither the first nor the last time Washington was spared by Cornwallis.[13]

On November 24, Washington's retreat continued south to Newark. Yet unaware of Lee's perfidy, he ordered Lee and his troops to join him unless some "new event" prevented him. Lee did not respond. Not receiving an answer, on November 27, Washington again wrote Lee, asking where he was and why he had not yet come. Still Lee did not respond. On December 10, Washington wrote yet another letter to Lee from Trenton. He needed Lee to prevent the British from taking Philadelphia. "I cannot but request and entreat you and this too, by the advice of all the Genl, Officers with me," wrote a rather desperate-sounding Washington, "to march and join me with all your force, with all possible expedition. The ultimate exertions . . . will not be more than sufficient to save Philadelphia . . . Do come on . . . and if it can be effected without delay, may be the means of preserving a city." And in the postscript, Washington urged, "Pray exert your influence and bring with you all the Jersey Militia you possibly can."[14] Lee, however, had other ideas.

On December 14, after receiving a communication from Lee explaining the delay as indecision over the route to take to join him, an exasperated Washington wrote, "I have so frequently mentioned our Situation, and the necessity of your Aid, that it is painful to me to add a Word upon the Subject, Let me once more request and entreat you to march immediately for Pitts Town."[15]

This letter never reached Lee. The day before a detachment of soldiers led by twenty-two-year-old Banastre Tarleton captured him as he dallied over a late breakfast at an inn at Basking Ridge. The small guard that accompanied him was easily overtaken. When Washington heard the news he wrote his cousin Lund, "Unhappy Man! Taken by his own Imprudence."[16] General Sullivan now took command of these troops and made his way to join the general.

The "imprudence" of Lee soon became obvious. When captured, he possessed a letter written to fellow General Horatio Gates. "*Entre Nous* [just between us] a certain great Man [Washington] is most damnably deficient," he opined. "If I stay in this province I risk myself and Army, and if I do not stay the Province is lost forever . . . In short, unless something which I do not expect turns up, We are lost."[17] The loss of Lee, the most experienced general in the army, eventually turned out to be a blessing for Washington. Congress soon granted him more authority and the comparisons of leadership with Lee ended.

Faced with troop desertions, enlistments ending, and lack of shoes and clothing for his men, Washington wanted to leave New Jersey and escape Cornwallis. He ordered all available boats to meet him at Trenton. Passing through Princeton, Washington arrived on December 3. Cornwallis trailed him but was ordered by Howe not to attack without the support of Howe's own troops.

Arriving on the sixth, Howe gave the Americans sufficient time to cross the Delaware. The next day, Howe slowly advanced to Trenton, arriving on the eighth. Washington thought better of confrontation and, one hour before the arriving British, ordered the evacuation of the twelve hundred rearguard troops. Local Tories informed Howe that if he hurried he could catch Washington, but again Howe let his quarry escape.

Charles Willson Peale, an American artist and eyewitness to Washington's crossing, was appalled by the sight of the American retreat. "It was the most hellish scene I ever beheld . . . The Hollowing of hundreds in their difficulties of getting Horses and artillery out of the boats, made it rather the appearance of Hell than any earthly scene," he recalled. Watching the Americans troop march by, he noted, "a man staggered out of line and came toward me. He had lost all his clothes. He was in an old dirty blanket, his beard long and his face full of sores . . . which so disfigured him that he was not known to me on first sight."[18] It was only after the man addressed him that Peale recognized his own brother, Ensign James Peale, one of the mere hundred survivors out of the one-thousand–strong Maryland regiment commanded by General William Smallwood. Such was the condition of Washington's tatterdemalion army as he crossed into Pennsylvania.

NINE

Trenton

Victory or Death.

—COUNTERSIGN FOR THE BATTLE OF TRENTON

DECEMBER 1776 WAS one of the most pivotal periods in the Revolutionary War. Washington faced two distinct major battles. On the one hand the British were only hours behind. On the other hand he faced the disintegration of his army and a lack of support from the civilian population. "We have had another convincing proof of the folly of short enlistments," wrote Nathanael Greene to Nicholas Cooke on December 4. "The time for which the five months men were engagd expird at this critical period. Two Brigades left us at Brunswick notwithstanding the Enemy were within two hours march and coming on. The loss of these troops at this critical time reduced his

Excellency to the necessity to order retreat again."[1] Events were about to happen quickly.

On December 12, Washington received a letter from Sam Adams letting him know Clinton's force of ten thousand were in Rhode Island. Could Washington spare a general officer, maybe Greene, to assist in their defense? Also on the twelfth Washington wrote Hancock that his intelligence had discovered troops nearby and, "Upon the whole there can be no doubt that Philadelphia is their object, and that they will pass the Delaware as soon as possible."[2]

The next day he received word from Sullivan of ". . . the loss of General Lee, who was this morning taken by the Enemy near Veal Town."[3] That same day Congress packed up and moved to Baltimore. The entire city of Philadelphia was in an uproar, fearing an invasion from Cornwallis's troops at Brunswick; this was only sixty miles down the King's Highway, one of the best roads in the country. Also on the thirteenth, unbeknownst to Washington, Howe decided to end his campaign and spend the winter in New York, leaving a regiment (primarily Hessians) at Trenton.

Washington believed both he and Philadelphia were under imminent attack. "The Delaware now divides what remains of our little force from that of Genl Howe whose Object beyond all question, is to possess Philadelphia," he wrote to James Bowdoin, a member of the Massachusetts Council, on December 18. In the face of incredible odds Washington's character and faith again showed through: "Upon the whole our Affairs are in much less promising condition than could be wished," he wrote in what could only be described as an understatement, "Yet I trust under the smiles of Providence, and by our own exertions, we shall be happy. Our cause is righteous and must be supported."[4]

"We are at present in a very disaffected part of the Provence," he wrote on the same day to his brother Samuel, "and between you and me I think our Affairs are in a very bad way." The problem was not so much Howe, but "from the defection of New York, New Jersey, and Pennsylvania—In short the conduct of the Jersey, has been most Infamous—Instead of turning out to defend their Country and affording aid to our Army they are making their Submissions as fast as they can." He reiterated Howe would "make an attempt upon Philadelphia this Winter." He needed reinforcements badly and quickly, and "if every nerve is not strained to recruit the New Army with all possible Expedition I think the game is pretty near up."[5]

If the campaign of 1776 was to be salvaged, if the nearly unbroken string of defeats was not reversed, and if the colonies did not rally, then the game certainly might have been up. But Washington was resilient and persistent. Even in this darkest hour an audacious plan was forming in his mind. The general needed something to not only rally his troops but also to reinvigorate the cause. In a matter of two weeks, the rest of his army might disappear. A popular revolutionary writer—coupled with a bold unexpected attack—soon kept the fledgling nation from despair.

Among the forlorn troops that escaped Fort Lee across the Delaware was a British-born writer who was making quite a name for himself. Thomas Paine was the author of the well known pamphlet, *Common Sense*. This forty-seven-page publication originally appeared in January 1776, and called for a separation between Britain and America. "'Tis time to part," Paine wrote, putting in plain language what many Americans believed. Paine had volunteered for service in the army in July and quickly became an aide to Nathanael Greene. As he marched and suffered with the men, Paine reflected upon what he observed. The revolution was at a crossroads and the cause might be lost. He decided to inspire the rebels—and those who were still on the fence—to action.

On December 19, the *Pennsylvania Journal* published the first of a series of tracts that would become known as *The Crisis*. The familiar words are as stirring now as when written:

> These are the times that try men's souls: The summer soldier and the sunshine patriot will, in this crisis, shrink from the service of his country; but he that stands it NOW, deserves the love and thanks of man and woman. Tyranny, like hell, is not easily conquered; yet we have this consolation with us, that the harder the conflict, the more glorious the triumph. What we obtain too cheap, we esteem too lightly;—Tis dearness only that gives every thing its value.[6]

Knowing the value of it, Paine made sure to describe Washington's character: "There is a natural firmness in some minds which cannot be unlocked by triffles, but which, when unlocked, discovers a cabinet of fortitude; and I reckon it among those kind of public blessings . . . that God hath blest him with uninterrupted health, and given him a mind that can even flourish upon care."[7] It was now up to that mind and character to inspire and lead the "shadow army," as Greene called it, to do its part.

On December 20, in the midst of a snowstorm, General John Sullivan brought the nearly 2000 troops formerly under Lee's command to Trenton. Washington expected four thousand. Many were in worse condition than Washington's own men. "So destitute of shoes that the blood left on the frozen ground, in many places, marked the route they had taken," described General Heath, upon viewing the poor souls.[8] Two days later, General Horatio Gates arrived with his remaining six hundred men; militia and local German volunteers added nearly another fifteen hundred. Upon this force of less than six thousand soldiers rested the future of American independence.

The same day Colonel Reed pressed Washington in a letter to make a bold move against the enemy. "Even a Failure cannot be more fatal than to remain in our present Situation," he counseled, "in short some Enterprize must be undertaken in our present Circumstances or we must give up the Cause."[9] Later that day, December 22, two sentries picked up a farmer from the New Jersey side of the river and brought him in for questioning. Surprisingly, Washington spent nearly thirty minutes alone with the man. Afterward he turned the man over to the guards, who locked him up. Later that night a suspicious fire began near the guardhouse. After putting out the fire, the sentry noted the prisoner had somehow escaped.

The escaped prisoner, John Honeyman, was one of Washington's spies. Posing as a Tory cattle dealer, he provided information about Colonel Johann Rall's Hessian disposition at Trenton. Honeyman assured Washington that no ships were being built to cross the Delaware and that Rall's unit was basically in a defensive mode, isolated, with supporting units miles away. Providing information to the rebels was only half of Honeyman's assignment. He was, in fact, a double agent. After his escape from the rebels, he reported to Rall that the Americans were so sick and weak they were incapable of mounting any kind of attack.[10]

The following day, Dr. Benjamin Rush visited Washington. He noted that the general seemed depressed and inattentive to his presence, but kept writing some words on bits of paper. When one of them fell to the floor Rush picked it up and read the words: *Victory or Death*. Rush didn't know it at the time but Washington had just given the countersign that put the Battle of Trenton in motion.[11]

"The bearer is sent down . . . to inform you that Christmas Day at Night . . . is the time fixed upon for our Attempt on Trenton," Washington responded to Reed on December 23. "For heaven's sake keep this to yourself," he added, "as the discovery of it may prove fatal to us, our numbers, sorry I am to say, being less than I had any conception of—but necessity, dire necessity will—nay must justify any Attempt."[12]

On Christmas Eve, Washington met with his leadership for the final briefing. His simple plan called upon his exhausted men to do the impossible. He would cross the Delaware with twenty-four hundred Continentals, including Greene, Sullivan, and Stirling. He chose McKonkey's Ferry, nine miles away from Trenton, as his crossing point. General James Ewing would take seven hundred across at Trenton and close off any escape route across Assunpink Creek. Finally, fifteen hundred troops under General John Cadwalader and Joseph Reed would go downriver to Bristol in case the commander there, Colonel Carl Emil Kurt von Donop, tried to reinforce Rall. It was a bold, heroic and potentially disastrous plan.

Knox would be in charge of the crossing, which would be made on large, flat-bottomed sixty-foot-long Durham boats. These vessels, designed to carry up to fifteen tons, were built to carry heavy bulky freight such as iron ore, whiskey or grain. They were canoe shaped at either end and drew only twenty inches of water, perfect for the eighteen cannon. Glover and his fishermen would again provide the oarsmen and supervision of these craft.[13]

Christmas Day saw men celebrating differently on both sides of the river. Washington's shoeless men wrapped their feet as best they could. Others cleaned their weapons. Washington ordered all to "cook rations for three days." They would begin the march to McKonkey's Ferry at about two p.m. The Germans, "who make a great deal of Christmas," would no doubt drink "a great deal of beer and have a dance tonight."[14]

Although the day began cold but clear, as soon as the march began the weather turned. Soon sleet, snow, and blowing rain moved in from the northeast. "It is fearfully cold and raw and a snow storm setting in," wrote one officer. "It will be a terrible night for the soldiers who have no shoes. Some of them have tied old rags around their feet; others are barefoot, but I have not heard a man complain."[15] Those at the end of the column followed bloody footprints left by those at the front. The crossing was made even more difficult because the blowing snow and chunks of ice now forming in the river impeded the boats.

Glover's men poled and rowed their way across the Delaware in the freezing, blowing wind.

The actual crossing took three hours longer than expected. Those who had crossed warmed themselves by large bonfires until all debarked. Washington crossed at seven o'clock and watched as time slipped by. The crossing was supposed to have been completed by midnight, allowing time to reach Trenton before daybreak. Yet it was not until 4:00 a.m. when the nine-mile march began. Washington considered retreat but rejected the idea as being more risky than continuing.

"It haild with great violence the Troops march'd with the most profound Silence and good order," wrote Henry Knox to his wife.[16] At the midway point Washington paused and "gave orders that every Officer's Watch should be set by his, and the Moment of Attack was fixed," detailed Captain William Hull. Washington then split his forces. Sullivan took his fourteen hundred men along River Road while Greene and Washington took the parallel Scotch Road. At 8:00 a.m., to blowing sleet and rain, the first shots were fired.

"It may have been an hour after daybreak," Lieutenant Andreas Wiederhold of the Knyphausen Regiment wrote in his diary. "I was suddenly attacked from the side of the woods on the road to John[son]'s [McConkey's] Ferry." He immediately ordered his seventeen men to return fire, believing this to be a minor skirmishing party. When he saw himself "surrounded by several battalions," he ordered a retreat. Washington described his troops' actions to Hancock, "The Out Guards made but small Opposition, tho', for their Numbers they behaved very well, keeping up a constant retreating fire from behind Houses." Thus began the Battle of Trenton.[17]

Confusion reigned as four thousand troops battled through the one hundred houses of Trenton. Due to the weather most muskets did not fire making it "mostly an affair of artillery, bayonet, sword, and spontoon [half pike]." Grapeshot cut down many of the Hessians as they fought to escape or confront their enemy.[18]

Henry Knox described the battle to his wife in a letter dated December 28. "We forc'd the guards & enter'd the Town with them pell-mell, & here succeeded a scene of war of Which I had often Conceived but never saw before. The hurry fright & confusion of the enemy was [not] inlike that which Will be when the last Trump shall sound." His cannon and howitzers had been placed at the head of the streets and the fleeing Germans ran right into them. Hurriedly they tried to form into a square on the plain but discovered they were surrounded.[19]

The fifty-six-year-old Colonel Rall himself tried to rally his men from horseback. "We presently saw their main Body formed," described Washington, "but from their Motions, they seem'd undetermined how to act."[20] Bravely leading his men against a force far superior to his, Rall's body suddenly shook from the impact of two musket balls piercing his chest and fell mortally wounded. His men, now leaderless, began fleeing in all directions. Perhaps five hundred Hessians managed to escape across Assunpink Creek until Glover and his men arrived to cut off their exit.

"Measures were taken for putting an entire stop to their retreat," wrote Knox, "by posting troops and Cannon in such passes and roads as it was possible for them to get away by—the poor fellows. After they were form'd on the plains saw themselves Completely surrounded—the only resource left was to force their way thro numbers unknown to them." The Germans were then forced to surrender with their artillery, "6 brass pieces arms Colors, &c. &c."[21] Washington recorded the surrender of 23 officers and 886 men. His casualties included two officers and two privates wounded. Accounts of how long the battle lasted differ, but most put the time at under one hour. "It is a glorious victory," recorded Stryker. "If he [Washington] does nothing more he will live in history as a great military commander."[22]

One of those wounded was Captain William Washington, a relative of the general. The other was the future president— Lieutenant James Monroe. He would be represented holding the flag in the famous 1850 painting by Emanuel Leutze. The twelve-foot high, twenty-foot wide canvas, entitled *Washington Crossing the Delaware*, is one of the best-known depictions of the Revolutionary War. It hangs today in New York's Metropolitan Museum of Art.

Discussion now centered on what to do next. Washington knew this victory, while stunning, must soon be followed by another. He wanted to press his advantage with an attack on Princeton. In this he was supported by Knox and Greene. Others recommended caution. The men were exhausted—having lost at least one night's sleep—and freezing. Some had also discovered the Hessian liquor cabinet and imbibed "great Quantities of Spirituous Liquors." In a more practical vein, the forces under Generals Ewing and Cadwalader had not all been able to cross the river, due to ice. Washington also recognized that since he was outnumbered by troops "below me, and a strong Battalion of Light Infantry being at Princetown above me, I thought it most prudent to return the same Evening."[23] At noon they began the nine-mile trek back to McKonkey's Ferry and again made the crossing. The weather had turned bitter, and nine hundred or so prisoners and all the loot caused this crossing to be even more difficult. Some of the inebriated fell into the river and eventually three froze to death. Washington and the cause, however, had a victory.

TEN

Princeton

We've got the old fox safe now. We'll go over and bag him in the morning.

—LORD CHARLES CORNWALLIS

THROUGHOUT AMERICA, NEWS of Washington's victory did much to encourage the cause. Many viewed this as God's protection and providence. The colonists' freedom was part of God's great plan and Washington was His agent. "What can't Men do when engaged in so noble a cause?" wrote Captain William Hull from Connecticut.[1] The enemy was less sanguine.

The British blamed the Hessians and inept politicians. Politicians blamed each other and the generals. In Europe the debate raged over the use of Hessian mercenaries. Meanwhile, in New Jersey, the Germans retreated from their positions at

Bordentown, Black Horse, and Mount Holly, as Washington praised his men and planned his next move.

"In justice to the Officers and Men, I must add, that their Behavior upon this Occasion, reflects the highest honor upon them," wrote a proud Washington to Hancock, summarizing the actions at Trenton on December 27. "The difficulty of passing the River in a severe Night, and their March thro' a violent Storm of Snow and Hail, did not in the least abate their Ardour. But when they came to the Charge, each seemed to vie with the other in pressing forward."[2] He did not have long to bask in the glow of victory. In four days enlistments of the New Englanders expired, leaving him with only fourteen hundred ragged Virginians.

Now located five miles west of McKonkey's Ferry in Newton, Pennsylvania, Washington used all his skills to preserve his forces. In his general orders of the twenty-seventh, he tried to both flatter and cajole his men into reenlisting. "The General, with the utmost sincerity and affection, thanks the Officers and soldiers for their spirited and gallant behavior at Trenton yesterday. It is with inexpressible pleasure that he can declare, that he did not see a single instance of bad behavior in either officers or privates." Indeed, he continued that if there was any fault to be found, "it proceeded from a too great eagerness to push forward upon the Enemy." His uncharacteristic gushing praise was followed by a reward. All of the booty that had been taken would be sold and the funds distributed. For a more immediate reward the commissary was "strictly ordered to provide Rum for the Troops."[3]

On the twenty-ninth, desperate to keep the advantage won

at Trenton, and hoping to inspire the men with more action, Washington again marched his men to the Delaware for yet another crossing. His plan was to take Princeton and press on to Brunswick, where the British treasury contained seventy thousand pounds sterling. Greene's men were able to cross on newly frozen ice below Trenton. Sullivan's troops at McKonkey's Ferry were not so fortunate. Forced to either break the ice or avoid ice chunks, the crossing took longer than expected. This time Knox had to ferry twice as many cannon.

On New Year's Eve, Washington addressed the New England men once more in a bid to keep them from leaving in the morning. They had served longer than any other regiment and recognized the hardships to come. He offered them a bounty of ten dollars for six more weeks of service. To the sound of a drum roll he asked for those who would heed the call to come forth. No one moved. Washington, visibly upset at the reaction again addressed the men. This account by a sergeant, penned almost fifty years later, gives the essence of what was said:

> My brave fellows, you have done all I have asked you to do, and more than could be reasonably expected. But your country is at stake, your wives, your houses, all that you hold dear. You have worn yourselves out with fatigues and hardships, but we know not how to spare you. If you will consent to stay but one month longer, you will render that service to the cause of liberty and to your country which you probably never can do under any other circumstances. The present is emphatically the crisis that will decide our destiny.[4]

Again the drum rolled. Men looked around and someone whispered, "I will remain if you will." Another stated, "We can't go home under these circumstances." Nearly all fit men stepped forward.[5] Washington was frankly gambling. He did not have the money to pay the bounty until the next day. Although the men looked ragged, weary, and more like scarecrows than soldiers, Washington had his army, which, with the infusion of some fresh Pennsylvanians, now numbered sixty-five hundred. He would make the most of it.

Washington learned another astounding fact that day: Congress had granted him almost unlimited powers over the military: "Resolve That Genl Washington shall be and he is hereby vested with full ample and complete Powers to raise and collect together in the most speedy & effectual Manner from any or all these United States sixteen Battalions," wrote John Hancock on December 27. Furthermore, he was "to take wherever he may be, whatever he may want for the Use of the Army." He was to determine the worth of said goods and pay for them in Continental currency. Otherwise, he could "arrest and confine Persons who refuse to take the Continental Currency, or are otherwise disaffected to the American Cause." In other words, for a period of six months, Washington had been given virtual dictatorial powers.[6]

Congress now knew, even before they had heard the news of his victory at Trenton, that the fate of the nation lay with Washington. The war was now his to win or lose. In a letter accompanying this resolution was written, "Happy it is for this country that the general of their forces can safely be entrusted with the most unlimited power, and neither personal security, liberty, nor property be in the least degree endangered thereby."[7]

"Instead of thinking myself free'd from all civil Obligations by this mark of their Confidence," he wrote back to Congress, "I shall constantly bear in Mind, that as the Sword was the last Resort for the preservation of our Liberties, so it ought to be the first thing laid aside when those Liberties are firmly established."[8] Washington may not have been tactically the most brilliant general, but trust in his honor and character was well placed.

Late on January 1, 1777, Washington learned that Lord Cornwallis, who had cancelled his homeward voyage to visit his ailing wife, had again taken charge in the field, and was on the move. Filled with confidence that he could easily defeat Washington, Cornwallis marched to retake Trenton. Washington sent messages to all his field commanders to report with their troops as soon as possible. "I expect your Brigade will be here by five O'clock in the Morning without fail," he wrote to Cadwalader. "At any rate do not exceed 6." Cadwalader missed the deadline by one hour, arriving at seven.[9]

By then Washington had formed a line behind the Assunpink Creek. This creek, with a chest-high depth, would not stop the British but could act as a kind of moat to slow them down. Knox covered the stone bridge with his forty cannon. Cornwallis and the Hessian commander Donop raced down the Princeton Road to confront the Americans. At Maidenhead, perhaps six miles from Trenton, Cornwallis was confronted by an advance party sent out by Washington to buy time for his men to get across the bridge. Under the command of an Irish-born Pennsylvanian,

Colonel Edward Hand, the riflemen did just that. Their "rifled" long rifles were much more accurate than the smooth bore muskets, and they fired with accuracy upon the British. A newly formed German immigrant regiment "gave way with very little Resistance," recorded Reed. It was not until after the sun had set, about five o'clock, that Cornwallis arrived at Trenton. He attacked just as the last of Washington's troops crossed the bridge.

After an initial attack on the lower ford failed, a unit of Hessian grenadiers made ready to charge the bridge. Frontal attack was their specialty. Initially composed of the largest, strongest men who could hurl bombs at the enemy, they were considered elite troops. The grenadiers' mission was to charge and take fortified positions, one of the most dangerous jobs in the army. This time they failed in the face of American firepower. "Well boys, you know the *old boss* has put us here to defend this bridge; and by God it must be done, let what will come,' admonished the Virginian colonel Charles Scott. "Now I want to tell you one thing. You're all in the habit of shooting too high. You waste your powder and lead, and I have cursed you about it a hundred times . . . whenever you see them fellows first begin to put their feet upon this bridge do you shin 'em."[10] In other words, killing a man only removed him from battle; a wounded soldier, however, required two more to carry him to safety. The orders worked, After suffering heavy losses, the grenadiers either retreated or surrendered.

Yet another attack upon the bridge soon followed. Artillery and concentrated fire mowed down the oncoming men. Still they charged. Gradually, those in the middle of the bridge had enough and stopped. Breaking ranks they fled back to cover as the Continentals, believing they had carried the day, gave a premature but prophetic rousing cheer.

"They came on a third time," wrote an American sergeant, "We loaded with canister shot and let them come nearer. We fired all together again, and such destruction it made, you cannot conceive. The bridge looked red as blood, with their killed and wounded, and red coats."[11] The number of casualties is uncertain, though it is clear the British and Hessian forces were soundly defeated. Washington's defensive strategy had worked brilliantly.

Cornwallis met with his leadership to discuss a possible night attack on the vulnerableAmerican position. Sir William Erskine, his quartermaster, urged an immediate assault. "If Washington is the general I take him to be," he argued, "his army will not be found there in the morning." Cornwallis, however, believing he had Washington trapped, decided to wait until daylight. "We've got the old fox safe now," he crowed. "We'll go over and bag him in the morning."[12]

The old fox had other ideas. At sunrise, just before 7:30, the British sentries looked at the American line. They saw no one. The fox had again made a spectacular night retreat and left the attackers stunned. Where was he and how had he done it once again?

This time the weather helped him. The night of January second saw a hard freeze. After consulting with his officers, Washington discerned the only way out was east. Using a partially cleared new road, Washington decided to go on the offensive and hit the British garrison at Princeton. Knox wrote his wife, "From these circumstances the General thought it was best to attack Princeton 12 miles in the rear of the enemys Grand army."[13]

Leaving a detachment of four hundred who kept fires burning and sounded like they were digging in with entrenching tools, the remaining six thousand quietly slipped away. Two cannon were also left to periodically but sporadically harass the enemy. The baggage was sent south to Burlington to allow for greater speed. Wrapping wheels with cloth and taking advantage of the hardened, frozen ground, the army marched up Quaker Road and planned to attack Princeton at daybreak. Three hours later the remaining four hundred would start down the road.

Early the next morning, Greene's lead column, led by General Hugh Mercer, encountered a force of British light horse nearly two miles from Princeton. Thinking they were just a reconnaissance force, Washington sent orders to attack. The battle that followed in Clarke's orchard, turned out to be much more than a skirmish.

Colonel Charles Mawhood had been left in charge of Princeton. He and two regiments were on their way to reinforce Cornwallis when they encountered the Americans. His troops immediately took cover and opened fire upon the advancing Americans. After firing several rounds, they fixed bayonets and charged.

Mercer, falling from his wounded horse and surrounded, used his empty musket as a club upon the approaching enemy. Quickly encircled, he was suddenly struck with the butt of a musket. Upon falling, he was run through seven times by British bayonets and left for dead. His brigade began a hasty retreat.

Colonel John Haslet tried to stem the retreat and was quickly felled with a bullet to the head. Panic now set in. If not for the artillery of Knox and the presence of Washington, who quickly rallied the troops and formed to confront the redcoats, the day might have ended in a rout.

Ordering his men not to fire until he gave the order, the two armies faced off at about thirty yards. "Halt!" he ordered, and then, "Fire!" Almost simultaneously the two volleys rang out. Washington was directly in the line of fire. John Fitzgerald, his aide, fearing his beloved general would fall, pulled his hat over his eyes. When the smoke cleared, however, Washington sat calmly on his horse calling for his men to charge the now fleeing British.[14]

"It is a fine fox chase, my boys!" the general roared as he led his tired men after them. His leadership and example quickly turned defeat into victory. "Washington's greatness was far beyond my description," wrote an officer later. "I shall never forget what I felt at Princeton on his account, when I saw him brave all the dangers of the field and his important life hanging as it were by a single hair with a thousand deaths flying around him. Believe me I thought not of myself."[15] Such was the adulation he received from his followers.

To escape the oncoming rebels, the fleeing redcoats took cover in Nassau Hall, one of the most secure buildings at the College of New Jersey (now Princeton University). Hamilton's artillery made short work of this resistance and about three hundred quickly surrendered. Some one hundred were left dead in the field. Losses for the Americans numbered forty-four. Especially felt, however, were the losses of Washington's good friend Hugh Mercer, who suffered for nine days before dying, and Colonel John Haslett.

Washington's men, "without rest, rum, or provisions for two nights and one day," were both tired and angry. They had seen Mercer brutally bayoneted, their comrades hacked to death, or their skulls crushed by redcoat musket butts, and they snapped. They took out their vengeance by looting the city and stripping the dead and wounded British. When Washington discovered the mistreatment of prisoners, he put a stop to it. He personally assisted some of the wounded to safety and others he sent to Dr. Rush for care.[16]

Eager to escape lest the oncoming reinforcements catch them at Princeton, Washington, after allowing about an hour for the men to loot supplies, blankets, and especially shoes, ordered a retreat. He desperately wanted to push on to Brunswick, nearly ten miles away, but after consultation with his officers, decided the men were in no condition to continue. "In my Judgment Six or Eight hundred fresh Troops upon a forced march would have destroyed all their Stores and Magazines," he wistfully wrote Hancock, "taken . . . their Military Chest containing 70,000 pounds and put an end to the War."[17]

On a positive note, the general continued that "The Militia are taking spirit and I am told are coming in fast." Unfortunately those from Philadelphia were not doing as well since they had sent their blankets off with the baggage to Burlington. Still, he added, "They have undergone more fatigue and hardship than I expected Militia (especially Citizens) would have done at this inclement Season."[18]

Several days later the exhausted men and their leader established their winter headquarters at Morristown, New Jersey. Although Washington at first considered it a temporary stay, he soon recognized the relative safety of the location and decided to remain. It was a wise choice. By the end of the winter, Washington's forces numbered nearly eight thousand.

Undoubtedly Washington now reflected upon how much the past few weeks had changed the future of the cause. On December 18 he had written his brother Samuel, "the game is pretty well up." But after inflicting stunning defeats at Trenton and Princeton, his troops rallied and did what many called impossible. His militia troops from around the country were turning into a unified force to be reckoned with. Shoeless, without blankets, and nearly naked, in the dead of winter they had pushed the enemy sixty miles from Philadelphia and cleared the west side of New Jersey. Furthermore, his troops now viewed him with awe. He had renewed confidence in both Greene and Reed after the Lee incident and they likewise saw him with new respect. His army accomplished head-to-head victories against not only the British redcoats, but also the professional, well-trained Hessians. Perhaps more importantly, he had stirred the nation. Through the inspiring words of Paine and the military leadership of Washington, the colonies again had hope.

Martha Washington

Washington and Lafayette at Valley Forge.

Martha Washington

ELEVEN

Brandywine

I suppose we shall have a very hot evening.

—Washington aide Robert Hanson Harrison

Throughout the winter of 1777, Washington maintained his camp at Morristown, where Martha joined him in March. Protected by the topography, he was in a good defensive position. He was also centrally located between the Hudson River—so he had quick access to either New York City or Albany—and the Delaware—so he could quickly be in Philadelphia. Howe comfortably wintered in New York City and kept strong positions at both Amboy and Brunswick, New Jersey.

As spring approached, the general faced several problems, especially disease. Smallpox returned in the winter with a vengeance. "We have done every thing in our power to hasten up the new Levies," wrote Congressman Richard Henry Lee from Baltimore in February 1777, "but the want of arms and cloaths, with the small pox, obstructs and delays us prodigiously."[1] Washington subsequently ordered all troops to receive inoculations. Conditions were much the same in Albany. "As soon as Dr. Potts arrives here," Major General Philip Schuyler wrote Washington, "I shall direct the Troops to be inoculated in the Manner you mention." Many used the epidemic as an excuse to desert, contributing to the usual problem of maintaining troop strength. The six-month enlistments obtained at Princeton would soon be up and recruiting was proceeding slowly.[2]

By May, however, things began to turn around. At the end of the month Washington had an army of nearly nine thousand. His five divisions were commanded by Major Generals Greene, Benjamin Lincoln, Stephen, Stirling, and Sullivan. Utilizing the authority given him by Congress in 1776, Washington reformed and streamlined his army. He professionalized the quartermaster, hospital, commissary, and ordnance departments. His personal influence and power had never been higher. Morale, like the weather, seemed to be improving on a daily basis. But where and when would Howe strike? Washington's intelligence service was woefully inadequate on this score.

Washington believed Philadelphia would be the military target for the campaign season of 1777, as Congress had returned to this city on March 12. "The designs of the Enemy are not, as yet, clearly unfolded, but Philadelphia I conceive is the object in view," wrote Washington to Virginia House of Delegates Speaker Edmund Pendleton on April 12.[3] Yet the northern frontier was also a possibility. "Gentleman Johnny" Burgoyne had captured Fort Ticonderoga and was threatening an attack down the Hudson Valley. Washington needed to remain flexible and mobile.

Howe's movements seemed to confirm Washington's suspicions. Encamped now at Amboy, Howe had accumulated a force of eighteen thousand. In June he marched closer to Philadelphia, pausing about halfway between Morristown and Trenton at Somerset Court House. Something about Howe's movements, however, raised red flags in Washington's mind. Why did Howe not carry his heavy baggage, his bridge and boat making equipment? Why were they traveling so lightly on a major expedition? Believing this action to be a ruse and possible trap, Washington repositioned his troops.

In May, Washington complained of another distraction. Foreign soldiers of fortune came to America to participate in the war and Congress provided them with commissions, even appointing two as colonels. "These men have no attachment or tyes to the Country," Washington wrote Congress, "further than Interest binds them—they have no Influence—and are ignorant of the language." Most significantly, however, "they have not the smallest chance to recruit others, and our Officers think it exceedingly hard, after they have toild in the Service, & probably sustaind many losses, to have Strangers put over them."[4] The one area where Washington thought commissioning foreigners, especially the trained French, might be a good idea was in the artillery or as engineers. He considered these essential and needed skills, but this was not the first time he had faced this mixed blessing of foreign assistance.

Several months before, in February, he had particularly singled out the French as being a problem. "They are coming in swarms from old France and the Islands," he complained to Hancock, and it was impossible to distinguish "Men of Merit . . . from mere Adventurers." But the French were also contributing more than warriors. "A Vessell is just arriv'd at Boston with 1200 Stand of Arms 1000 Barls of Gun Powder, from France," added Washington in a postscript to General George Weedon in March. In addition to this, some British prizes taken in the West Indies, which included arms cannon and dry goods, had arrived in Philadelphia. "Good News this," closed the General.[5]

Perhaps the best contribution to the American army arrived on August 1. On that day, Marie Joseph Paul Yves Roch Gilbert du Motier, the Marquis de Lafayette, met Washington. The nineteen-year-old had received a congressional commission the day before as a Major General, but with no command. Although he spoke almost no English and had never seen battle, he was extremely wealthy, served at his own expense, and had influence in France. Washington took an immediate liking to the engaging, eager youngster.

Lafayette came seeking both revenge and glory. He blamed the British for the death of his father in the French and Indian War. As a young, idealistic adventurer he would become one of Washington's strongest supporters and demonstrate great bravery in the upcoming campaigns.

The British and American forces played cat and mouse for the early part of the summer. In July, Howe's troops boarded 260 ships and set out under the command of Lord Richard Howe, for no one knew where. Although Washington recognized the need for an American navy he was powerless to do anything about it. A challenge to British naval dominance would have to wait until the French could be persuaded to join the fight. He was frustrated with an enemy that could disappear over the horizon and suddenly appear at any point without warning. Finally, on August 21, Washington received reliable intelligence that the fleet was in Chesapeake Bay.[6]

In an attempt to bolster recruitment and calm the fears of those in Philadelphia, now the perceived goal of Howe, Washington marched his roughly twelve thousand-man army through the streets of the city. Like many generals to follow, he did not want to miss an opportunity to impress civilians by parading his troops. The general orders for August twenty-third included, "The army is to move precisely at four in the morning [the actual march began at 7:00] . . . The army is to march in one column thro' the City of Philadelphia . . . great attention [is to be] given by the officers to see that the men carry their arms well, and are made to appear as decent as circumstances will admit." Since there was no common uniform, each appeared in his regimental colors if possible. Still concerned with desertion, he added, "and if any soldier shall dare to quit his ranks, he shall receive Thirty-nine lashes at the first halting place afterwards."[7]

The general was leaving nothing to chance. In the eighteenth century, every army had a number of female camp followers. These included men's wives, lovers, washerwomen, cooks, seamstresses, and prostitutes. Everyone recognized they were a part of the army, but "Not a woman belonging to the army is to be seen with the troops on their march thro' the city," read the orders. The drums and fifers were to gather and play "a tune for the quick step played but with such moderation, that the men may step to it with ease; and without dancing along, or totally disregarding the music, as too often has been the case." Also to ensure all was proper, "The men are to be excused from carrying their Camp Kettles tomorrow."[8]

Howe's army landed at Head of Elk (near present day Elkton, Maryland) on August 25. The men and animals had been cramped into ships for more than a month, and needed time to restore themselves to fighting trim. For fresh food they foraged the countryside, raiding and stealing cattle, sheep, and even horses. Although Washington, accompanied by Greene and a few guards, rode on ahead and observed these actions, they were helpless to prevent the plunder. On September 8, Howe's thirteen thousand-strong force moved towards Philadelphia. In a countermove, Washington deployed his troops to the east side of Chadds Ford on the Brandywine Creek and established his headquarters at the home of a Quaker, Benjamin Ring.

The morning of September 11 dawned foggy and damp. By about seven o'clock the fog had burned off and the day turned hot and humid. Baron Wilhelm Knyphausen, commander of all German troops in America and now commanding one of Howe's "grand divisions," initiated the first significant action at Chadds Ford. His mission was a feint designed to make Washington commit his men. Washington was not fooled and this engagement turned out to be an artillery duel.

Washington correctly perceived that Howe's main objective

was to turn his right flank. Shortly after eleven o'clock, the general received a report from Colonel Moses Hazen that a large enemy contingent was moving to the north on Great Valley Road. Washington sent Colonel Bland to confirm this intelligence. Soon after, a second messenger confirmed the information that "a large body of the enemy, from every account five thousand, with sixteen or eighteen field pieces marched along this road [Great Valley] just now."[9] Washington now believed Howe had made a mistake and split his forces. The divisions of Stephen and Stirling could defend the right flank. He would attack Howe's remaining troops across the ford with Greene's and Sullivan's divisions. Before he could implement these measures, however, he received another contradictory message from Sullivan. There were no troops in the north.

Confused, Washington ordered everyone to halt until he received additional information. Early that afternoon the news came by means of a patriot farmer, Squire Thomas Cheyney. The hatless, coatless, out-of-breath farmer informed the general that he had been scouting himself and the Continentals were about to be surrounded. This bombshell stunned Washington, who must have looked doubtful. "I'd have you know I have this day's work as much at heart as e'er a blood of ye!" cried Cheyney. He then proceeded to draw a map and show where he had encountered the enemy. Apparently Washington still appeared dubious, causing the farmer to yell, "You're mistaken, General. My life for it you're mistaken. By hell! It's so. Put me under guard 'til you find out it's so."[10]

It was so. Howe knew of fords across the river that Washington did not. Just like Brooklyn Heights, Howe discovered an unguarded access to Washington and took advantage of it. Soon after two o'clock, Sullivan sent word that the enemy was approaching him from the rear. The situation now looked different. Instead of Washington catching Howe with his troops split, it might be he who was in the trap. Across the river to his front was Knyphausen with his five thousand; attacking his rear was Howe with his eight thousand. Since the actual situation was unclear, Washington ordered Sullivan to meet Howe; he and Greene with the divisions of Wayne and Maxwell would remain flexible.

Just over two hours later, Washington heard the sound of cannon and musket fire to his rear. Almost simultaneously the artillery fire in front of him quickened. "At half after 4 o'clock the enemy attacked General Sullivan at the ford next above this," dictated Washington to his aide, Robert Hanson Harrison. "A very severe cannonade has began [sic] here too, and I suppose we shall have a very hot evening."[11]

Washington decided that he and Greene were going to help Sullivan. Galloping on and being led by a local, Joseph Brown, whom he had to chivvy along, Washington arrived before Greene's forces. The only one who had beat him there was the young Lafayette. Upon arriving Washington quickly grasped the situation. Sullivan's left was buckling under the pressure and falling back to Plowed Hill. The rest of the line was sagging, with Hessian and British units pressing hard at the center. Trying to rally his troops as he had done before, Washington rode up and down the line accompanied by Lafayette. Although tired from marching fifteen miles that day, the British were determined. They outnumbered the Americans by more than two-to-one.

"Cannon balls flew thick and many and small arms soared like the rolling of a drum," wrote one Continental commander.[12] It was no use. The rebels began to flee.

With General Weedon's Virginians, Greene arrived with his thirteen hundred men less than an hour after Washington. The scene they witnessed upon arrival was appalling. As they advanced they came face-to-face with their own fleeing comrades. They were forced to make a path to allow those retreating to pass before they could even fire. Greene and his men fought a slow retrograde operation, holding up the British as long as possible. Because of their efforts the majority of the beaten army was able to escape.

The scene at Chadds Ford was just as bleak. Knyphausen had achieved success in crossing the Brandywine. The fighting was intense, with grapeshot and musket ball bringing many to their death. One officer of the Queen's Rangers described it, "The water took us up to our breasts and was much stained with blood." Wayne's Pennsylvanians and Maxwell's light infantry brigade met on the road to Philadelphia. There, both forces began the long slow retreat to the capital city.[13]

Many have described the Battle of Brandywine as one of Washington's poorest showings in the war, as he again exhibited those traits that made him a failure in New York. He failed to adequately reconnoiter the terrain, trusting others with a job he himself should have done. Since the area was populated by a large number of loyalists, Howe had the better intelligence. The outcome, however, did not affect his reputation. In fact it was Sullivan who was blamed with the "Folly and misconduct" that had cost them "the Glory of a Compleat Victory."[14] Although Washington discouraged this type of criticism of his officers (he was too much of a gentleman for that), neither did he correct it. It was a victory for Howe, who had outmaneuvered and outfought his opponent, but Washington and his army had escaped to attempt to save the threatened Philadelphia another day.

TWELVE

Germantown

Be firm, be brave, shew yourselves men, and victory is yours.

—GEORGE WASHINGTON

THE DAY AFTER the defeat at Brandywine found Washington down but not out. Even as he slowly made his way to Philadelphia, he was devising a plan to stop Howe's seemingly inexorable march. On this date he ordered General Smallwood to take advantage of the situation by "falling on the Enemy's Rear and attacking & harrassing them, as Often as possible." He just needed support and "a Spirited Effort by the people would in all probability put a happy & speedy end to the present contest."[1]

The next day in his general orders, Washington assured the men he had confidence that "In another Appeal to Heaven (with the blessing of providence, which it becomes every officer and soldier humbly to supplicate) we shall prove successful."[2] To buck up their flagging spirits, he also ordered thirty hogsheads of rum to be distributed at one gill (four ounces) per day. That same day, September 13, they crossed the Schuylkill River and made camp near the Quaker settlement of Germantown. For the first time in a week the men were able to put up their tents for shelter. To keep the capital free from occupation, Washington had to prevent Howe from crossing the Schuylkill.

The crucial events of the next few weeks, culminating in the Battle of Germantown, were largely determined by two unavoidable natural events—rain and fog—and two commonplace articles—shoes and an inopportunely placed stone house.

After resting his troops for four days, Howe pressed on toward his prize: Philadelphia. Discovering the American position at Paoli, he sent a party to probe their line. Then the rain began to fall.

In letters to Hancock on both the nineteenth and twenty-third, Washington explained what happened. "When I last recrossed the Schuylkill it was with the firm intent of giving the Enemy Battle wherever I should meet him," he wrote. "The two Armies were upon the point of coming to a general Engagement but were prevented by a most violent Flood of Rain all the day and the following Night."[3] Suffering through this deluge, he discovered that the forty rounds of ammunition allotted to each man were soaked and useless. Fearing British occupation, the rebels had moved much ammunition and supplies out of the city to

Reading, northwest of the city. Thus, Washington had to force march his troops there to resupply and on the eighteenth they received fresh cartridges.

His men then trudged back south to defend both Swede's Ford and Fatland Ford, located about half a mile from Valley Forge. The deluge had caused the river to swell and Washington hoped this would slow down Howe. Washington also ordered Wayne and his Pennsylvanians to harass the enemy rear. Wayne, not waiting for help from Maxwell as ordered, decided to continue to Paoli and reconnoiter the enemy lines. Two days later, just after midnight, he was surprised by five British regiments. With fixed bayonets the British made short work of the sleeping men, leaving perhaps three hundred killed and many more wounded or captured.

By mercilessly forcing his men to march and eventually to cross the rapidly flowing Schuylkill on the twentieth, Washington put himself in a good position. He was now prepared to defend both of the main fords and keep Howe on the opposite side of the river. What happened next, however, was another example of the wily veteran Howe taking advantage of the learn-as-you-go Washington.

On the twenty-first, Continental scouts reported the British were on the move north. Believing that Howe was again attempting to "turn his right," Washington pondered his next move. Should he follow the enemy on a parallel course to prevent him from crossing north of him? Or was this a feint? If Howe continued his present course he would soon be in Reading and could capture all the American supplies stored there. On the other hand if Washington moved with him, the fords would be unprotected. He decided to follow Howe.

It was a feint. The enemy made it across the river and on the twenty-sixth marched into Philadelphia. At great personal risk, the members of Congress—considered outlaws or traitors by the British—had to flee again, this time west to York. Most colonial supporters had already fled, leaving Tories and Quakers to cheerfully receive the British. The general would later place the fault of his misjudgment and the subsequent loss of the capital on three factors: The enemy's movements confused him. He had no spies in the area. His men could not return and chase the enemy because of lack of shoes.

The enemy moved "by a variety of perplexing Maneuvers," as he described the loss to Hancock, "thro' a Country from which I could not derive the least intelligence being to a man disaffected, contrived to pass the Schuylkill last Night at the Flat land and other Fords in the Neighborhood of it." Upon receipt of this information, Washington decided "by the advice of the General Officers" to wait until the next day to chase them. Although he awaited reinforcements from New England, the strongest reason he decided to wait was "the want of shoes." He added that "at least one thousand Men are bare footed and have performed the marches in that condition." Hearing that there were a lot of shoes in Philadelphia "in the hands of private people," he advised Hancock he had sent for them.[4]

Recognizing he had lost Philadelphia, Washington made a wise tactical decision. He recognized that the city, one hundred miles up the Delaware from the Atlantic, could only be adequately supplied by shipping. To prevent this happening he had begun a series of small forts along the river, and had placed obstacles such as *chevaux-de-frise* in the river. If he could stop the supply of goods on the river he certainly could do it on land. Because of this he was "not yet without hope that the acquisition of Philada may, instead of his [Howe's] good fortune, prove his Ruin."[5] To this end he sent artillery and troops to Fort Mifflin, Red Bank (Fort Mercer), and Billingsport. Although this strategy would ultimately prove ineffective against the mighty British navy and superior land forces, it did tie up British land and naval forces for a time.

Howe also recognized the strategic necessity of keeping the Delaware open. He placed Cornwallis in charge of Philadelphia, sent two regiments to assist in clearing the river, and settled the majority of his men in Germantown, just outside the capital. In so doing he had reduced his total number of troops to about eight thousand. Washington noticed this and consulted with his generals.

Now that he had received reinforcements from the east, his army numbered more than eleven thousand. On the twenty-eighth he met with his council of war. As usual, Washington wanted to make a "general & vigorous attack." The others were not so sure. Their decision was to proceed toward the garrisons at Germantown and then make a decision.

While Washington was being outmaneuvered in Pennsylvania, good news was coming from the northern campaign. The colonial forces there, under the command of the snobbish and irritating General Horatio Gates, defeated the forces of "Gentleman Johnny" Burgoyne at Freeman's Farm, New York. This came on the heels of a previous victory at Bennington, in what is now Vermont, which had boosted American morale and cut off vital supplies for Burgoyne. The victory also contrasted Washington's failures with Gates's successes. Now eager for a battle to bolster his own reputation, on October 2 Washington moved his men closer to Germantown. After another council with his generals, the decision for battle was made.

As he prepared for the upcoming battle, Washington used a combination of praise and sectional rivalry to motivate his depressed men. First he referred to Gates's success in the north. "This surely must animate every man," he proclaimed in his general orders on the third, "This Army—the main American Army—will certainly not suffer itself to be out done by their northern Bretheren—they will never endure such disgrace." The same heroic spirit that motivated the New Englanders surely beat in their breast. "Covet! My Countrymen, and fellow Soldiers! Covet! a share of the glory due to heroic deeds! Let it never be said that in a day of action, you turned your backs on the foe—let the enemy no longer triumph."[6]

Washington also had a problem with desertions. Howe promised deserters would be welcomed in his army and farmers who turned to the Tory cause would receive protection. This had not happened, however. "A few dastard souls accepted the disgraceful boon," Washington informed his army, "But his promises were deceitful—the submitting and resisting had their property alike plundered and destroyed." Howe left them "no choice but Conquest or Death . . . Be firm, be brave, shew yourselves men, and victory is yours," he promised.[7]

The plan for the battle, like that at Trenton, involved splitting the American forces. The army still did not all have the same uniforms so they placed a piece of white paper in their hats for identification. Greene and Smallwood commanded the left wing and had the farthest to move. Washington, along with Sullivan and Armstrong, departed nearly two hours later. Not only did darkness slow the movement but also the oncoming, ever thickening fog.

Sullivan's troops were the first into the battle. At Mount Airy, perhaps a mile north of Howe's main body, they skirmished with a small party of sentries. Surprised at the arrival of the Continentals, and thinking them but a small party, they charged. Not knowing what was coming their way, Sullivan's men panicked and retreated, halting only when they ran into Sullivan and reinforcements. Now the British began to retreat to Germantown. The fog continued to deepen.

Out of the fog Howe appeared, yelling at his men to stand and form—but the whistling sound of passing grapeshot caused their commander to turn and flee himself. "I think I never saw people enjoy a discharge of grape before," one of the British officers remembered, "but we really all felt pleased to see the enemy make such an appearance, and to hear the grape rattle about the commander-in-chief's ears, after he had accused the battalion of having run away from a scouting party." Howe rode off immediately, "full speed."[8]

As Sullivan continued his pursuit of the retreating British, his men suddenly realized someone was firing at them from the rear. Amidst the pea-soup fog, made worse by the smoke from the musket and cannon fire, he noticed a two-and-a-half-story stone house. This was Judge Benjamin Chew's residence, now deserted. Or so Sullivan had thought. A fleeing regiment of infantry under Lieutenant Colonel Thomas Musgrave were barricaded in this house and were causing havoc among the oncoming Continentals.

After a parley among his chief officers, Washington decided to take the house. Although Alexander Hamilton and others urged him to go around it and continue the attack, he agreed with Henry Knox who voiced the opinion "it would be unmilitary to leave a castle to our rear."[9] Knox then brought up his four small field pieces. The artilleryman either overestimated the strength of his pieces or underestimated the thickness of the stone walls. The three and six pound cannonballs could not penetrate the stone. Meanwhile Musgrave's muskets were taking their toll. After nearly an hour of artillery pounding with no effect, and American casualties reaching nearly one hundred, Washington called off the attack.

Suddenly, off to the east, Washington heard musket fire. Had Greene arrived or was this another attack by the enemy? It is difficult to get a clear picture of what happened next. Confusion reigned in the murky fog. Not knowing who was where caused friendly fire casualties. Soon Sullivan's panicked troops emerged out of the fog fleeing for their lives. Officers, including Washington, tried to stem the fleeing troops but to no avail. Cornwallis entered the scene with three fresh battalions and chased Greene's retreating forces for five miles but then stopped and let them escape.

The retreating army had been forced to march nearly forty

miles in twenty-four hours, most without food. The lack of water was also a problem. Private Martin was "tormented with thirst all the morning, (fighting being warm work) . . . ."[10]

About two weeks later, Washington summed up the battle. "After a hot contest of two hours and forty minutes of a glorious decision . . ." he wrote Landon Carter, "and being as we thought upon the point of grasping victory, it was snatched from us by means altogether unaccountable." The fog and smoke of battle "rendered impossible, at times, to distinguish friend from Foe at the distance of thirty yards which caused our Men I believe to take fright at each other."[11]

Although the battle was decidedly a victory for the British, it had the surprising effect upon Washington's men of raising morale. "Upon the whole our men are in high Spirits," he wrote Jonathan Trumbull, "and much pleased with the fortune of the day."[12] They had nearly beaten the disciplined British in the field. They had almost won. Had it not been for the fog, and the distraction of Chew's house, they might have pulled off a victory.

A more significant battle was decided in the north. On October 17 in Saratoga, New York, to the tune of "Yankee Doodle," Burgoyne surrendered his sword in defeat to Gates. As previously determined, Gates handed it back to him. As Burgoyne departed the area, Gates was forced to assign troops to physically protect him, as some locals wanted to add tar and feathers to "Gentleman Johnny's" immaculate uniform.

Colonial success, however, did not extend to the river forts. Slowly yet inexorably, the British navy and Howe's forces cleared the river of American defenses. By November 21, the last vestiges of the attempt to close the Delaware were removed. Now fully open to resupply, Philadelphia became the comfortable winter quarters for Howe and his mistress, the wife of his commissary general, Mrs. Elizabeth Loring.

Washington was left to ponder his next move. Would Howe leave the comfort and security of Philadelphia to come after him? Or would he simply be content to enjoy the social life in the city? What to do and where to go? Washington was sure his troops could not remain in the exposed condition at Whitemarsh, Pennsylvania. These immediate pressing problems faced the army.

The surrender at Saratoga and the resistance at Germantown set international wheels in motion. On December 17, 1777, the French announced to the American envoys that they were prepared to recognize American independence and supply men, arms, and, most importantly, naval support to their new allies. This action proved crucial to the outcome of the American Revolution, but sadly for Washington, it was not immediately felt.

THIRTEEN

Valley Forge

If George Washington be not a man of God, I am greatly
deceived.

—QUAKER FARMER POTTS

"I AM SICK, discontented, out of humor. Poor food. Hard
lodging. Cold weather. Fatigue. Nasty clothes. Nasty cookery.
Vomit half my time . . . Here comes a bowl of beef soup—full of
burnt leaves and dirt, sickish enough to make a hector spue—
away with it boys . . ."[1] So one surgeon described conditions at
the place Washington set up camp on December 12. After leaving
Whitemarsh, Washington crossed the Schuylkill and arrived at
was what was called the Gulph. Congress wanted the Continental
Army between their location in York and the British army. It was a
miserable place; "starvation here rioted in its glory," commented

a sarcastic Private Martin. This was not the place to winter and Washington knew it. Before leaving and moving to more permanent quarters, Washington addressed the troops.[2]

"Tomorrow being the day set apart by the Honorable Congress for public Thanksgiving and Praise; and duty calling us devoutely to express our grateful acknowledgements to God for the manifold blessings he has granted us," read the general orders for December 17, "the General directs that the army remain in its present quarters, and that the Chaplains perform divine service with their several Corps and brigades." Furthermore he exhorted them with the assurance that soon "Huts may be erected that will be warm and dry."[3]

On the nineteenth, Washington chose a permanent place to winter only seven miles from the Gulph, selecting a two-mile-wide area just south of the Schuylkill River. Located about twenty miles from Philadelphia, surrounded by woodlands for building material, and protected by rolling hills, it was a good defensive choice. The Valley Creek that provided water had previously powered an iron forge, hence the name Valley Forge.

Even as he set up camp, Washington was only too aware of how poorly provisioned his men were. Asking for help in the form of clothing for his Connecticut men, he wrote the governor of that state, Jonathan Trumball: "We must expect to lose a considerable number of men by sickness . . . in the course of the winter." He was right. By the end of the winter, twenty-five hundred men—fully a quarter of the troops—would die from sickness, starvation, and exposure.[4]

Only two days after arrival the troops let their officers know how they felt about their condition. Especially galling was the lack of suitable food. In a near mutiny the emaciated men hollered, "No Meat! No Meat!" They had only "fire cake and water."[5] Washington got the message loud and clear. Upon learning that a British patrol was in the vicinity, Washington roused his men. "I ordered the Troops to be in readiness . . . when behold! to my great mortification," he wrote the then president of the Congress, Henry Laurens, "I was not only informed, but convinced, that the Men were unable to stir on account of provision, and that a dangerous mutiny, begun the night before and which with difficulty was suppressed by the spirited exertions." Recognizing the lack of provision had a serious impact upon combat readiness, if not the very existence of the army, he resolved to investigate the food situation personally.[6]

After an inspection of the commissary, he discovered "That he had not a single hoof of any kind to slaughter, and not more than 25 Barrells of Flour," to feed over ten thousand men. "I am now convinced beyond a doubt, that unless some great and capital change suddenly takes place in that line [the commissary], this Army must inevitably be reduced to one or other of these three things. Starve—dissolve—or disperse."[7]

Washington immediately sent out foraging parties but with few results. Gruel or "fire cake," a pasty mix of flour and water cooked on hot rocks, remained the main source of sustenance. The "no meat" situation continued.

Food was not the only concern. No decent clothing since Brandywine had come. Most had only one shirt and many had no blankets or shoes. "We have by a Field return this day made, no less than 2,898 Men now in Camp unfit for duty, because they are barefoot and otherwise naked," he informed Congress. Sickness was becoming a pressing issue.[8]

"I need not inform your Excellency that we have now upwards of 5,000 Sick in our hospitals," wrote Dr. Benjamin Rush on December 27. As bad as the illness was, medicine and space for treatment was woefully inadequate. "I have seen 20 sick men in One room ill with fevers & fluxes, large eno' to contain only 6, or 8 well men without danger to their health," continued Rush. His advice was that good food and fresh air were the best remedy for the ill. Air was plentiful; food was not.[9]

Washington had always been a stickler about not pillaging the locals. Although the British did this on a large scale, he insisted his men pay for what they needed. By February, however, the food situation was desperate. In addition, he heard the British were expected to come into the area to confiscate what little there was. "It is of the utmost Consequence that the Horses Cattle Sheep and Provender within Fifteen or Twenty miles . . . be immediately removed," he ordered Greene, in order "to prevent the Enemy from receiving any benefit therefrom, as well as to supply the present Emergencies of the American Army." The result was food enough for just a few days.[10]

Sometime during the winter of 1777, a Quaker named Isaac Potts was walking through the forest when he heard a human voice. Cautiously he approached and observed Washington kneeling in prayer. After watching the general finish his devotions and depart "with a countenance of angel serenity," Potts rushed home to tell his wife. "All's well. All's well!" He exclaimed,

"George Washington will yet prevail." After explaining what he saw to his surprised wife, Potts declared he had always thought the sword and Christianity were incompatible. But, "If George Washington be not a man of God," he expressed, "I am greatly deceived." Furthermore, he expected God, "through him, [to] work out a great salvation for America."[11]

Washington ordered the men to build shelters for themselves. Twelve men were assigned to build and live in a cabin 14 feet long, 16 wide, and 6.5 feet high, resulting in 18 square feet for each. Most paid little attention to these orders. They made shelter out of whatever they could find.

Not only were the enlisted men in bad condition, but even Washington's officer corps was disintegrating. "It is matter of no small grief to me," he wrote General Weedon, "to find such an unconquerable desire in the Officers of this Army to be absent from Camp, as every day exhibits." Because of their absence, "I must attempt (for it can be no more than an attempt) to do all these duties myself." Officers at every level were requesting furloughs; some never returned. "If every Officer would lay his hands properly to the work," he lamented to Weedon, "& afford those aids which I have a right to expect, and the Service requires instead of longing, & hankering after their respective homes," he could endure. Knox and Greene, whose wife, Caty, joined him, remained loyal. Giving him some comfort, Martha arrived on February 5.[12]

To Washington's great frustration, it was not only the natural elements that caused suffering. It was bureaucratic corruption, incompetence, and inefficiency. Several of the officials in charge of the acquisition and distribution of food and clothing were simply not doing their jobs. These were congressional appointees, bureaucrats who could not be voted out of office. They had little supervision and had built their own little fiefdoms at the expense of the troops.

Food and clothing were available. The local farmers had meat and produce, but instead of selling it to the starving Continentals, who paid in continental dollars, which were practically worthless, they sold to the British, who paid in pounds sterling, hard currency. Loyalists also hoarded or hid goods from the colonial troops sent out to buy supplies.

Commissary General of Purchases William Buchanan was especially inefficient. In a letter to Buchanan, one commissary advised him about what Washington thought of him. "In conversation with his Excellency to day on the Subject of Supplies he expressed himself as follows—Dam it what is that reason Mr Buchanan is not here does he think to indulge himself at home whilst we are distressed and suffering for want of provision. This is Language that his Excellency is by no means accustom'd to use and you may Judge of the provocation when he is oblig'd to adopt." Yet since Buchanan and the others were not in the military chain of command, they did not need to respond.[13]

During the month of January 1778, Washington undertook one of the most significant and far-reaching actions of his career to date—to reform the entire military structure. Asking advice from his generals and utilizing all of his past military experience, he wanted to streamline and make more efficient what he saw as a dysfunctional organization. On January 29, he completed his plan and sent the thirty-eight-page document to Congress. The result would reform the structure of the army.

One recommendation was the draft. Patriotism alone could not fill the ranks of the army. Those so motivated were already serving, thus some other measure was necessary. One means was "that of filling the regiments by drafts," he suggested. "This is a disagreeable alternative but it is an unavoidable one." Recognizing the unpopularity of such a measure he specified, "As drafting for the war, or for a term of years, would probably be disgusting and dangerous, perhaps impracticable, I would propose an annual draft of men, without officers, to serve 'till the first day of January, in each year."[14]

His ideas incorporated top-to-bottom reforms. He urged streamlining and combining units, reforming the quartermaster system, hospital and sanitation departments, pay and promotion changes, military police, uniforms, and alliances with Indians, all of which came under his scrutiny with the goal of a totally integrated and unified military. Four months later, and with some modifications, Congress adopted the new standards for the Continental Army.[15]

In addition to his immediate practical military difficulties, Washington also had political challenges. During the previous year's campaign, while he was suffering losses at Brandywine, Germantown, and the forts along the Delaware River, Gates was having success in the northern campaign. Some in Congress, especially from the New England delegation, wanted to make Gates the new commander in chief.

"The Northern Army has Shewn us what Americans are

capable of doing with a *General* at their head," wrote Benjamin
Rush anonymously to Patrick Henry; "The Spirit of the Southern
Army is no ways inferior to the Spirit of the northern. A Gates—a
Lee, or a Conway would, in a few weeks render them an irresist-
able body of men."[16]

In January, Congress received a long rambling tirade entitled
"Thoughts of a Free Man" about the state of the army and why
war continued. After expressing the poor condition of the army,
he challenged Washington's leadership and believed the nation
had deified him. "That the Head cant posobly be sound when the
whole body is disordered. That the people of America have been
guilty of Idolatry by making a man their god—and that the God
of Heaven and Earth will convince them by wofull experience
that he is only a man. That no good may be expected from the
standing Army untill Baal & his worshipers are banished from
the Camp—I beleive that. Verte [truthfully]."[17]

Lafayette viewed this dispute as serious and wrote
Washington about it. "Stupid men who without knowing a Single
word about war undertake to judge You, to make Ridiculous
Comparisons; they are infatuated with Gates," was Lafayette's
response to this criticism. In his opinion, and he still spoke for
many in the country, "I entertained the Certitude that America
would Be independent in Case she would not loose You. Take
a way for an instant that Modest diffidence of Yourself (which,
pardon my freedom, my dear general, is Sometimes too Great,
and I wish You Could know as well as myself, what difference
there is Betwen You and Any other man Upon the Continent,)
You Shall See Very plainly that if You were lost for America,

there is no Body who Could keep the army and the Revolution for Six months."[18]

In the military, much of the anti-Washington faction focused on the actions of General Thomas Conway, an Irish-born Frenchman who had come to America as a mercenary. Congress had recently appointed him inspector general, which technically put him in a position to oversee the actions of Washington. "What a pity there is but one Gates," Conway wrote to Gates. "But the more I see of this army, the less I think it fit for general action under its actual chiefs and actual discipline."[19] By the time Washington received word of this communication, attached as a note from Lord Stirling, the words had been twisted to read, "In a letter from General Conway to General Gates he says, 'Heaven has been determined to Save your Country; Or a Weak General and bad Counsellors would have ruined it.'"[20]

Shocked by what he viewed as disloyalty within his own ranks yet not wanting to add fuel to the fire, Washington wrote a curt note to Conway. "Sir: A Letter which I received last Night contained the following paragraph." He then quoted the note verbatim. Conway replied that he had written no such thing: "my opinion of you sir without flattery or envy is as follows: you are a Brave man, an honest Man, a patriot, and a Man of great sense."[21] Washington let the issue drop. The loyal Greene, however, smelled a conspiracy.

"What will be done with Conway, I don't know," wrote Greene to General McDougall; "he has but small talents, great ambitions, and without any uncommon spirit or enterprize." In addition to being great in his own eyes, the public had been given a false perception of Conway's abilities. Greene believed they wanted Washington ousted: ". . . this is done by a certain faction that is said to be forming under the auspices of General Gates and General Mifflin, to supplant his Excellency from command of the Army and get Genl Gates at the head of it."[22]

It is not really clear if there was such a conspiracy, which some historians have labeled the "Conway Cabal." What is clear, however, is that there was frustration and disappointment about how the war was going and Washington's overall leadership. To his credit, Washington stuck to his guns, tried to take the criticism in stride, and pressed on with his duties. A lesser man might have gotten caught up in the bickering and spent much time defending himself. Yet consistent with his humility, he submitted to Conway's inspection of the camp at Valley Forge. Although Washington admitted to not receiving him "in the language of a warm and cordial Friend," he wrote Laurens (he had never been good at "dissimulation"), and Conway was "received & treated with proper respect."[23]

The problem would soon disappear. Congress decided to stick with Washington. Gates and Mifflin were soon terminated with the Board of War. Conway lost his job as inspector general, and all three were reassigned to the army. In time, Gates and Washington would soon have a peaceful working relationship.

In February 1778, General Nathanael Greene reluctantly accepted the appointment as quartermaster general to replace the incompetent Mifflin, having been prevailed upon by both Washington and Congress. It was a wise choice. He immediately began to fix the broken system of supply using his abilities as an organizer and leader, and he ended much of the corruption and inefficiency that had nearly destroyed the Continental Army at Valley Forge.

On February twenty-third, there arrived another foreign adventurer who would change forever the way the army functioned. Forty-eight-year-old Friedrich Wilhelm Augustus von Steuben, a bona fide baron (yet now penniless), had been an officer in the Prussian Army serving under Frederick the Great. He knew how to drill and he knew about discipline. He could not, however, speak English. To translate for him he brought a seventeen-year-old boy who spoke French and English. A native German speaker, von Steuben had to translate in his head to French and give orders to the boy, who then translated them into English. In March 1778, Washington appointed him to train and discipline the Continental Army.

The baron began by emphasizing the fundamentals. Choosing one hundred of Washington's best men, he formed a model company and began drilling them while others observed. Soon he had them marching in step, standing at attention, parrying the bayonet, and maneuvering as an ever larger unit. It wasn't long before von Steuben had the entire army of seven thousand marching in unison.

Instead of using the usual harsh European form of discipline, von Steuben seemed to understand what worked with Americans. "Explain with mildness what the soldiers are to do; they are not to use them ill," he ordered his officers. "Point out their Faults patiently . . . there will be no other punishment for the soldier . . . than to make him exercise a whole hour after the others have done." His methods worked. Far from resenting the German, they chuckled at his cursing their ineptness in three languages. The nearly naked Continentals were also amused by his uniform. Wearing a resplendent Prussian officer's uniform, with a medal covering half his chest, the bespectacled von Steuben, his pet greyhound by his side, must have appeared exotic. Yet as the men felt increasingly good about themselves, and consistently improved from what some called "a mob" to an effective fighting force, his foreign nature became irrelevant. He was getting results that would soon save lives.[24]

Word of the French alliance announced the previous December made its way across the ocean, and on May 5, 1778, Washington told his men about it. "It having pleased the Almighty ruler of the Universe propitiously to defend the Cause of the United American-States," proclaimed the general orders of that date, "by raising us up a powerful Friend among the Princes of the Earth to establish our liberty and Independence upon lasting foundations, it becomes us to set apart a day for gratefully acknowledging the divine Goodness & celebrating the important Event which we owe to his benign Interposition."[25]

The orders further stipulated that after a prayer service, the discharge of cannon, and the men marching in formation, "Upon a signal given, the whole Army will shout *Huzza*! 'Long Live the King of France'—The Artillery then begins again and fires thirteen rounds, this will be succeded by a second general discharge of the Musquetry in a running fire—*Huzza*!—'And long live the friendly European Powers'—Then the last discharge of thirteen Pieces of Artillery will be given, followed by a General running fire and Huzza! 'To the American States.'" Each man was then given a gill of rum with his dinner to celebrate the day.[26]

A starving, naked, shoeless army had entered that Pennsylvania valley in December of 1777. In June 1778, a new, stronger army emerged, forged in hardship, and strengthened in body, soul, and spirit. The new quartermaster general Greene had provided the men with the physical necessities of life. Von Steuben's training had built an *esprit de corps*, instilling discipline, and providing new skills soon to be proven. Washington, by his stirring example, had continued to raise the spirits and provide a sense of purpose that, at least temporarily, dissipated the attitude of rebellion. In addition, the new organizational structure conceived by Washington and approved by Congress on May 27, 1778, provided military efficiency and structure. Because of these improvements, an entirely new army marched out of Valley Forge in June. The question was—where would it next strike the enemy?

Washington at prayer.

Washington crossing the Delaware.

Emanuel Leutze ©1898, Courtesy of the Library of Congress

FOURTEEN

Monmouth

[I have never seen]
so superb a man . . .

— MARQUIS DE LAFAYETTE

WASHINGTON HAD AT least three options as he contemplated emerging from Valley Forge. The first involved doing nothing, simply continuing to train and strengthen his forces. The second was to drive the British out of their comfortable existence in Philadelphia. The third, and this was Washington's inclination, was to retake the crucial city of New York. King George III—and the French—made the decision for him.

His Majesty was not pleased with Lord Howe. Why had he not forced this ragged band of upstarts to capitulate to the finest fighting force in the world? The king, listening to hawks led by

Lord Germain, was more determined than ever to keep America in his empire. He ordered Howe back to England to provide an explanation. The more aggressive Sir Henry Clinton, who had often disagreed with Howe, assumed command while Howe left for London in May of 1778.

Meanwhile French involvement in the war changed the worldwide tactical situation for Britain. Both Britain and France had colonies in the Caribbean. The British controlled the richest sugar-producing islands in the West Indies, including Jamaica and Barbados. Smaller islands such as Dominica, St. Kitts, Nevis, and Montserrat were lightly defended and obvious targets for the French. Some in the island colonies wanted to join the Continentals in revolt, but the fear of slave rebellions stopped them. Defending these islands from the French and other European powers would strain the British navy and suck troops from the northern army.

In April 1778, General Charles Lee, who had previously tried to undermine Washington's authority, rejoined Washington at his camp. Lee—a prisoner of war since December of 1776—had finally been traded for a British general and was back on active duty. Although Washington welcomed him, he was unimpressed when Lee arrived accompanied by his pack of dogs and a British mistress.

There was more news. Washington was told that the British were preparing to leave Philadelphia. To make certain, he dispatched Lafayette and twenty-two hundred men to make a reconnaissance, report any movement, and establish a spy system. "You will remember that your detachment is a very valuable one," he counseled the Frenchman, "and that any accident happening to it would be a severe blow to this army. You will therefore use every possible precaution for its security, and to guard against a surprise. ”[1] Lafayette chose Barren Hill, located roughly midway between the capital and Valley Forge, as a bivouac. This was an unwise position as Matson's Ford, nearly two miles to his rear, was the only way to cross the Schuylkill River, in case he needed to escape.

Through their own scouts, Howe and Clinton learned of Lafayette's position and attempted to exploit it. Sending out a force more than three times that of Lafayette, they soon cut off all visible means of retreat and were about to draw the noose on the Frenchman. But Lafayette had personally reconnoitered the terrain; perhaps he had learned from the mistakes of his mentor Washington. Leading his men through a nearly hidden trail, he safely escaped the snare and returned to safety. Von Steuben's training proved invaluable as the men retreated in a tight, orderly fashion. Although Lafayette had erred, he had, however, learned a valuable lesson in troop placement.

As predicted, on June 17, amidst a searing heat, Baron Knyphausen left Philadelphia with an advance guard to secure the bridge across the Delaware. The next day Clinton and the rest of the British forces began their evacuation. The twelve-mile-long train consisted of an army ten thousand strong, fifteen hundred wagons loaded with plunder, fearful loyalists with their possessions, and thousands of camp followers. The exodus took nearly the entire day. By the late afternoon, the Continentals were back in charge of the city with Benedict Arnold as commandant. Henry and Lucy Knox also came to Philadelphia, "but it stunk so abominably that it was impossible to stay there . . ."[2]

Also on June 17, Washington convened a council of war to discuss strategy, especially how to confront the retreating British. He asked the generals a series of questions and asked them to submit their answers in writing. A few days later he learned Clinton had moved into New Jersey. Before even receiving all the responses, Washington ordered the army to march.

Washington soon realized Clinton planned to march through New Jersey to New York, so the Continental Army set out to follow and harass Clinton along the way. Recalling his experiences with the Indians in the Ohio Valley nearly twenty-five years before, he expressed his strategy to Major General Philemon Dickinson. "I take the liberty of giving it to you . . . that the way to annoy, distress, and really injure the Enemy on their march (after obstructing the Roads as much as possible) . . . is to suffer them to act in very light Bodies . . . the Enemy's Guards in front flank and Rear must be exposed and may be greatly injured by the concealed and well directed fire of Men in Ambush," he counseled. "This kind of Annoyance ought to be incessant day and Night and would I think be very effectual."[3] This harassment soon proved effective as the unrelenting heat, lack of water, combined with the sniper fire, soon caused desertions among the British.

On June 24, Washington again convened his council. After a briefing on the current situation of both Continental and British troops, the general asked if this might "be adviseable for us, of choice, to hazard a general action?" Most of the council, including Lee, recommended caution, but not Greene or Lafayette. "If we suffer the enemy to pass through the Jerseys without attempting anything upon them," wrote Greene to Washington, "I think we shall ever regret it . . . People expect something from us and our strength demands it." Washington concurred and ordered four thousand troops into battle.[4]

Washington offered command of the troops to his second in command, General Lee. Thinking it unworthy of his talents or position, Lee refused; Lafayette, however, accepted with joy. As the battle loomed and Lee saw how large the force was and how significant the upcoming contest appeared, he changed his mind. "[It] is undoubtedly the most honourable command next to the Commander in Chief," he cooed in a letter to Washington, "my ceding it woud of course have an odd appearance, I must intreat therefore, (after making a thoushand apologies for the trouble my rash assent has occasion'd to you) that if this detachment does march that I may have the command of it." If Washington allowed Lafayette to command, "both Myself and Lord Steuben will be disgrac'd." Washington, ever one to use the chain of command to support his officers, relented. He soon regretted this decision.[5]

June 26 saw the heat-prostrated and weary British troops arrive at Monmouth Court House. Cloudless skies allowed temperatures to hover around the 100 degree Fahrenheit mark. The troops suffered horribly. Those famous red coats were made out of wool. As well, each man carried his own kit in a pack that could weigh sixty pounds. Moreover, the "harassing militia" had poisoned water wells along the way. Clinton decided the men needed a day to rest. Besides, he was spoiling for a fight in the open with the Continentals. The next day, the twenty-eighth, he got his wish.

Early that morning Lee ordered his men to move toward Clinton's rearguard. Washington gave him no specific orders; just march on and engage the enemy. This he did. Soon, however, he found himself in a predicament. The rearguard was being reinforced with about six thousand troops under Clinton. Tactically, he was in a bad defensive spot. His army was scattered and communication was difficult. Finding themselves in small isolated units, and facing a superior foe, Lee's troops began to retreat. Although not the panicked rout that might have occurred before von Steuben's training, the retreat became general. Overheated, thirsty soldiers wanted out.

Washington approached the scene on his white charger and was puzzled. He asked a retreating fifer what was happening. After receiving the answer that he was running from the enemy, Washington became enraged. This anger increased when two other soldiers told him Lee had ordered the retreat. Washington called for Lee.

Upon finding the somewhat dazed, retreating general, Washington demanded to know what he was doing. His response was that new intelligence had forced him to change plans. He then petulantly added that, in his opinion, this battle ought not to have been fought. Washington angrily answered that he was to follow orders, and reminded him he had insisted on leading the operation. Some accounts read that Washington "swore that day til the leaves shook on the trees" and called Lee a "poltroon." Whatever took place, Washington then assumed command.[6]

Typically, he immediately charged into the thick of it. "The commander in Chief was everywhere," wrote Greene. "His Presence gave Spirit and Confidence and his command and authority soon brought everything into Order and Regularity."[7]

Alexander Hamilton, another of Washington's aides, was nearly killed in the action when his slain horse fell on him. "I never saw the general to so much advantage," Hamilton recalled. "His coolness and firmness were admirable. He instantly took maneuvers for checking the enemy's advance and giving time for the army . . . to form and make a proper disposition." Lafayette reported he had never seen "so superb a man" as the general.[8]

Washington ordered the fleeing men to form a line overlooking what was known as the Middle Ravine. Charging back and forth, rallying his troops, directing his officers, Washington determined to make a stand. The ensuing battle lasted an hour and became especially bloody as the two forces met bayonet to bayonet. Slowly the Continentals retreated across a bridge until their artillery took over with enfilading fire.

Private Martin, an eyewitness, recounts a story of a woman, Mary Ludwig Hays, who assisted her husband in the artillery service. "While in the act of reaching a cartridge and having one of her feet as far before the other as she could step," he recounted, "a cannon shot from the enemy passed directly between her legs." This did no more harm than ripping her lower petticoat. Undeterred, she nonchalantly remarked, "It was lucky it did not pass a little higher" because if it had, "it might have carried away something else, and ended her and her occupation." Because this tobacco-chewing woman of no education, who smoked, and "swore like a trooper," carried water to the soldiers, they nicknamed her Molly Pitcher.[9]

The British also had artillery and after a two-hour-long duel, Clinton again attacked. The carnage was terrible, as wave after wave fell to cannon fire. Bayonet fighting again occurred, but this time the well-trained Continentals stood up to even the feared and respected Black Watch Highlanders. By 6:00 p.m. heat had also taken its toll. Many on both sides died from thirst and heat exhaustion. Clinton, believing nothing else could be accomplished, withdrew toward Monmouth away from the American guns. The battle was over.

That night Clinton stole a page from Washington's book. Leaving his campfires burning, around midnight his army silently retreated to Monmouth and then on to Sandy Hook. He left his nearly 250 dead on the battlefield. Almost a quarter of them had died of heatstroke.

"The Commander in Chief congratulates the Army on the Victory obtained over the Arms of his Britanick Majesty yesterday," stated the general orders on the twenty-ninth, "and thanks most sincerely the gallant officers and men who distinguished themselves upon the occasion." Especially recognizing the role of the artillery, Washington added, "the Commander in Chief can inform General Knox and the Officers of Artillery that the Enemy have done them the Justice to acknowledge that no Artillery could be better served than ours."[10]

Two days after the battle, Washington brought charges against Lee, who responded with a questioning letter. "They [your words and actions] implyed that I was guilty either of disobedience of orders, of want of conduct, or want of courage," Lee complained. "Your Excellency will therefore infinitely oblige me by letting me know on which of these three articles you ground your charge—that I may prepare for my justification which I have the happiness to be confident I can do to the army, to the Congress, to America, and to the world in general." In a final appeal to flattery, Lee continued, "I ever had (and hope ever shall have the greatest respect and veneration for General Washington) I think him endowed with many great and good qualities, but in this instance I must pronounce that he has been guilty of an act of cruel injustice . . ."[11]

The day he received Lee's letter, Washington responded: "Sir, I received your letter . . . What I recollect to have said, was dictated by duty and warranted by the occasion. As soon as circumstances will permit, you shall have an opportunity, either of justifying yourself to the army, to Congress, to America, and to the world in General; or of convincing them that you were guilty of a breach of orders and of misbehaviour before the enemy on the 28th Inst. in not attacking them as you had been directed and in making an unnecessary, disorderly, and shameful retreat. I am Sir your most obt servt."[12]

In December 1778, Congress suspended Lee and in 1780 he was cashiered from the army.

Clearly Washington believed he had won the battle at Monmouth. Although historians generally view it as a draw at best, Washington and the Continental Army made their point. They were no longer running scared. Their formations proved strong; they demonstrated their bayonet-wielding abilities. They had stood face-to-face with British regulars and not backed down. They had proven that their artillery was second to none. Surely it was indeed a "New Army" that emerged from Valley Forge.

FIFTEEN

The Road to Yorktown

We were absolutely, literally starved.

—PRIVATE JOSEPH PLUMB MARTIN

ON JULY 4, 1778, Washington ordered a celebration. His army was now in New Brunswick, New Jersey, and he still hoped to retake New York. On the heels of what he considered a great victory at Monmouth, he was in a festive mood. "Tomorrow, the Anniversary of the Declaration of Independence, will be celebrated by the firing thirteen Pieces of Cannon and a *feu de joie* of the whole line," read the general orders of July third. "The Soldiers are to adorn their Hats with *Green-Boughs* and to make the best appearance possible." Undoubtedly more importantly to the men, he ordered a "Double allowance of rum will be served out." The next day these orders were amended to read that after a thirteen-gun salute, "Perputual and undisturbed Independence to the United States of America," would be shouted three times.[1]

Both Benedict Arnold, the new commandant in Philadelphia, and the French Admiral Charles Hector, comte d'Estaing (recently arrived with his fleet off the coast of Virginia), sent him congratulatory letters. "[I] am very happy to hear the Enemy have suffered so very considerably in their march thro' the Jerseys," wrote Arnold on the eighth. "I make no doubt this Campaign will be crown'd with success, & that your Excellency will soon enjoy in peace the Laurels you have with so much perseverence, toil & hazard reaped in the Iron field of War."[2]

"I have the honor of imparting to Your Excelly the arrival of the King's fleet; charged by his Majesty with the glorious task of giving his allies the United States of America the most striking proofs of his affection," wrote d'Estaing upon his arrival on the eighth. "Accept Sir, the homage that every man—that every military man owes you; and be not displeased, that I solicit . . . a friendship so flattering as yours."[3] Surely only good things could happen now that the French fleet of sixteen warships and four thousand troops were on the scene.

The first crack in the American–French alliance did not take long to appear. D'Estaing had a poor reputation among his French naval colleagues and the reason was soon obvious. His cross-Atlantic trip had taken eighty-seven days, a long voyage, even for that time. Soldiers were packed on board like sardines. It was not unusual for up to half of the soldiers and crew to arrive sick, usually with scurvy. On a voyage in 1780, a Bavarian baron wrote about his trip in which he had a "large compartment" that he shared with nineteen others. The compartment was a total of 180 square feet, and 4.5 feet high. He described it as "not too comfortable" and, in addition to the noise, the "exhalations and other bad odors produced by the passengers" must have been quite an experience. These were the officer quarters. What could the troop accommodations have been like?[4]

Arriving off the coast of New York too late to meet Clinton's departing fleet, the admiral discovered his vessels had too deep a draft to enter the harbor. Next he sailed to Newport, in British-occupied Rhode Island, the home of Nathanael Greene. Greene suggested an attack on the British occupation forces by the Continental Battalion, commanded by Christopher Greene, a distant relative. The First Regiment of this battalion contained black troops and was the only unit larger than company size to integrate.

How did slave-owning Washington feel about blacks in the military? As previously noted, he was none too keen to allow freedmen to enlist. On October 8, 1775, he had put a question to his generals: "Whether it will be adviseable to re-inlist any Negroes in the new Army—or whether there be a Distinction between such as are Slaves & those who are free?" They had "Agreed unanimously to reject all Slaves, & by a great Majority to reject Negroes altogether."[5]

Thus in his general orders of November 12, 1775, Washington ratified this council's wishes. "Neither Negroes, Boys unable to bare Arms, nor old men unfit to endure the fatigues of the campaign, are to be inlisted."[6] However, he hadn't known that Lord Dunmore, the governor of Virginia, had issued an edict that any slave leaving his master and joining the British would receive his freedom. When Washington learned of this "diabolical scheme," he wrote Richard Henry Lee, "nothing less than depriving [Dunmore] of life or liberty will secure peace to Virginia." Grudgingly, Washington acquiesced to allowing freedmen to enlist.[7] As the war progressed, the need for troops forced state enlistment officers to fill their quotas by enlisting blacks. Maryland allowed slaves to gain freedom for service while others allowed slaves as substitutes for their masters. This usually resulted in their subsequent freedom.

In January 1778, Rhode Island general James Mitchell Varnum, suggested a way to increase enlistments in his state. "It is imagined that a Battalion of Negroes can be easily raised," he wrote. "Should that Measure be adopted, or recruits obtained upon any other Principle, the Service will be advanced." The next month the Rhode Island Assembly voted to enlist black, mulatto, and Indian freedmen into segregated units. Four months later they rescinded the order.[8]

All in all, it is estimated that between 5 and 6 percent of the Continental troops were black—about five thousand in total. Nearly the same number served with the British. After the war, these men were allowed to migrate to Canada. Disliking the climate, however, many moved to Africa where they formed the new state of Sierra Leone. American freedmen also traveled to Africa in 1819, forming the neighboring state of Liberia.

Washington was a practical man and needed troops, but

he was also a slave owner. Like most white southerners in this period, he feared arming slaves or free blacks. In a culture where the minority of whites controlled the majority of blacks, fear dictated principle. While his views may have matured over time, the reality is he did not free his own slaves until his death.

New Hampshire native General John Sullivan was placed in charge of coordinating with the French during the Rhode Island campaign. This was not a wise decision. Nathanael Greene, who wanted the job and had worked on planning the expedition, would have been a better choice. "You are the most happy man in the World," he wrote Sullivan in July 1778. "You are the first General that has ever had an opportunity of cooperating with the French forces belonging to the United States."[9]

The plan was for d'Estaing to drop anchor off the tip of Newport and bombard the British defenders. Meanwhile Sullivan and his ten thousand men, joined by four thousand French marines, were to come in on either side. Just as the attack was about to start, Admiral Howe appeared with a British fleet, causing the cautious d'Estaing to board his marines and pursue him. Sullivan was left to fume and sit out a violent three-day storm. Seeing the French depart, many militia deserted.

Three days later the battered French fleet returned. Both the storm and the British had taken their toll on the ships. D'Estaing, deciding he needed repairs before he could support Sullivan, sailed for Boston. Sullivan was furious. "General Sullivan very imprudently issueed something like a censure in General

Orders," wrote Greene to Washington on August 28; "indeed it was an absolute censure."[10] This signaled a decided cooling of the hopes the initial news of French assistance had evoked. Indeed, Sullivan's attitude quickly spread and was directed at all French—even Lafayette—who had been sent to Rhode Island to translate and assist in the action.

"I did not choose to trouble your friendship with the sentiments of an afflicted, injur'd heart," wrote Lafayette to Washington, "and injur'd by that very people I came from so far to love and support." Asking forgiveness for being so blunt, Lafayette continued, "frenchmen of the highest characters have been expos'd to the most disagreable Circumstances, and me, yes, myself the friend of America, the friend of General Washington, I am more upon a warlike footing in the American lines, than when I come near the british lines at newport."[11]

Washington had to do something quickly lest the cause be affected negatively by French withdrawal. He needed the French navy to disrupt British control of the seas. He also needed the supplies, manpower, and money they brought. To repair the breach between Sullivan and the French he fired off a letter. "Permit me to recommend in the most particular manner," he wrote Sullivan, "the cultivation of harmony and good agreement, and your endeavors to destroy that ill humor which may have got into the officers."[12]

Washington again turned to Greene to assist him in repairing the fracture with the French. "I depend much upon your temper and influence," he wrote Greene, "to conciliate that animosity which I plainly perceive, by a letter from the Marquis, subsists

between the American Officers and the French in our service."
Working together with Lafayette, they made it apparent to the
French that Sullivan—not all Americans—was the problem.[13]

Conceding there was little to be done for the rest of this campaign year, Washington moved his camp to Middlebrook, New
Jersey, for the winter. It was a much easier winter than the previous one at Valley Forge, and betrayed none of the bitter hardships
to come in the next year's quarters. During the winter, he continued training his army, rested, and hoped for better results in
1779.

The war saw relatively little advancement in the northeast during the year 1779. The British and French navies dueled in the
Caribbean. The British were securely ensconced in New York
and without French naval support, an American attack was considered unwise. Washington's attention turned, therefore, to the
western frontier, where King George had been arming and supply-
ing the Indians. Because of the trouble stirred up by the natives,
Washington allowed many of the local militia to remain near their
homes, thus depriving his army of much-needed manpower. Now
was the time to send a punitive expedition into the area.

General John Sullivan was placed in charge of twenty-five
hundred troops and ordered to meet up with General James
Clinton and his fourteen hundred. Their mission was to put an
end to the Indian and Tory raids in upstate New York. This was
not an exercise in pacification. Washington ordered "the total
destruction and devastation of their settlements." Harking back

to his frontier days during the French and Indian War, he advised Sullivan how to fight. Offense was better than defense and when there was opportunity, "rush on with the war [w]hoop and fixed bayonet—Nothing will disconcert and terrify the Indians more than this." Although there were few pitched battles, Sullivan did destroy forty small native settlements and thereby brought peace to the region.[14]

The British also were not completely inactive. On July 1, they sallied out of New York City, sailed about twenty-five miles up the Hudson, and took King's Ferry. Located some twelve miles south of West Point, this ferry connected Stony Point on the west bank and Verplancks Point on the east. While the British controlled New York, this position was the safest southernmost crossing of the Hudson for the Continentals.

Washington reacted by leaving Middlebrook and established his camp between the British and West Point. General Anthony Wayne made a brilliant night attack against Stony Point and captured over five hundred prisoners. Recognizing his position there was vulnerable, Washington moved his army to West Point. The only other engagement occurred in late August, when Major Henry Lee Jr. stormed a small garrison at Paulus Hook on the Hudson near Manhattan and took 158 prisoners before retreating.

With winter approaching the general had to make a critical decision—where to encamp. He chose Morristown, New Jersey. Departing West Point in late November, the army arrived on December 2, 1779, amidst snow and hail. It was a harbinger of the winter to come, which proved to be one of the coldest in history.

The eleven thousand or so soldiers immediately began building huts. Eventually there would be one thousand huts cleared from six hundred acres of trees. "Our army is without Meat or Bread; and have been for two or three days past," wrote Greene in early January. "Poor Fellows! They exhibit a picture truly distressing. More than half naked, and above two thirds starved."[15] Private Martin wrote, "We were absolutely, literally starved; I do solemnly declare I did not put a single morsel . . . into my mouth for four days and as many nights."[16]

Conditions grew so dire that Washington had little choice but to allow the men to plunder and forage. "The present situation . . . is the most distressing of any we have experienced since the beginning of the War," he wrote to the Magistrates of New Jersey on January 8. "For a Fortnight past the Troops . . . have almost been perishing for want. They have been alternately without Bread or Meat, the whole time . . . But they are now reduced to an extremity no longer to be supported." Their hunger "prompted the Men to commit depredation on the property of the Inhabitants which at any other period would be punished with exemplary severity, but which can now only be lamented." He told the magistrates if they failed to levy a quota on each county to feed the troops, "fatal consequences may ensue."[17]

The citizenry responded and brought cattle, flour, and, perhaps most importantly, teams to clear the roads and thus allow fresh supplies to get to the camp. "They gave the earliest and most chearful attention to my requisitions, and exerted themselves for the Army's relief in a manner that did them the highest honor," reported Washington to Congress on January 27. "They more than complied with the requisitions in many instances, and owing to their exertions, the Army in a great measure has been kept together."[18] The snow continued and the supplies dropped off, however, and by spring of 1780 things grew desperate again.

Existing only on bread crusts for days and going five months with no pay was too much for one Connecticut brigade. On May 25, 1780, they mutinied, mishandled some officers and threatened to go home. Fortunately, loyal Pennsylvania troops intervened and the mutiny died down. At the same time, news reached Washington that General Benjamin Lincoln had surrendered his entire army to Clinton in Charles Town, South Carolina, on May 12.

Washington had other problems of his own. After hearing of Clinton's victory and the Connecticut mutiny, Baron Knyphausen wanted in on the action; on June 6 he crossed into New Jersey. News from Tories and deserters had led him to believe he would be welcomed, but it was wishful thinking—the militia drove his forces back to Elizabethtown. There he was joined by the returning Clinton, whose troops crossed on pontoon bridges from Staten Island and set up camp in Springfield.

Upon hearing of Knyphausen's venture, Washington ordered the bulk of his troops to move toward West Point, where he believed the main British attack was aimed. He believed the attack on New Jersey was a feint. He left Greene with the rearguard and was marching away when he heard those forces under attack. Greene sent him a message that he was under heavy attack from a reinforced British force. Washington turned and drove his men hard to support Greene. The British fled and subsequently Washington discovered Knyphausen had left Springfield and returned to New York.

Although Washington was concerned about leaving the fourth largest city in the colonies in British hands, he began to wonder if perhaps the British were overextended. For an army to subjugate a country, it must not only have the forces to conquer but also to occupy and, at that time, North America was a large land area with a decentralized population. Even though the British had taken New York and Philadelphia, the population of the countryside was not subdued. Washington began to realize the opportunities that lay before him.

SIXTEEN

Victory

An Ardent Desire to spare the further Effusion of Blood will
readily incline me to listen to such Terms for the surrender of
your Posts and Garrisons.

—GEORGE WASHINGTON

ON JULY 10, 1780, a French fleet under Jean-Baptiste
Donatien de Vimeur, comte de Rochambeau, arrived in Newport,
Rhode Island. He promptly announced to the citizenry that a
much larger force was on the way. This was the news Washington
had waited for; together they could finally force the British out
of New York. Although not sure it was a good idea, calling it
"something Don Quixotal," the ever-loyal Greene began acquir-
ing supplies for the mission.[1] Washington learned Clinton had
set out with troop transports—ostensibly to attack Rochambeau

in Newport. He immediately determined to assist. Meanwhile Greene, offended by an investigation into his actions as quartermaster general, had resigned from the army. In view of the present situation, however, Washington begged him to stay until his replacement, Timothy Pickering, could learn the ropes.

As Washington crossed the Hudson he learned Clinton was returning to New York. He retreated to New Jersey and awaited the arrival of the second French fleet. On August 25, Washington heard from Rochambeau that a French frigate had brought arms and powder but that the second fleet was blockaded at Brest, unable to leave.

On September 8, Washington wrote Rochambeau to set up a date for a meeting at Hartford, Connecticut, and informed him of yet another disaster. "We have just received the most disagreeable advices from General Gates," he wrote, "of a defeat of the Army under his command near Camden in South Carolina the 16th of last month; in which the greatest part of his best troops were cut off."[2] In fact the entire army was lost, the third such loss in the South in the last two years. Now more than ever Washington believed that taking New York was the key to ending the war.

The meeting with Rochambeau, on September 20, accomplished little. There were simply too many unknowns. "We could only combine possible plans on the supposition of possible events," complained Washington, "and engage mutually to do everything in our powers against the next campaign."[3] Leaving on the twenty-third with Lafayette, Knox, and his staff, Washington decided to go by West Point and check with its commandant, Benedict Arnold, to see how defenses were coming. He was in for quite a surprise.

While Benedict Arnold had been the military commandant of Philadelphia from 1778 to early 1780, he'd met Major John André, a young ambitious British officer who was then head of British secret intelligence. Married to a woman with Loyalist leanings and unhappy with the progression of his military career in the Continental Army, Arnold began to think seriously about changing his allegiance to King George. He was also in debt due to a lavish lifestyle. To change his situation, he sought command of West Point with the express intention of selling the plans for the fort to the British—he had already begun selling information regarding troop location and strength to the British. Major André became the go-between, and was subsequently caught behind American lines—disguised as a colonial "John Anderson"—with incriminating papers.

Not yet aware of this, Washington sent his aides ahead to Arnold at West Point with the message that he would be there for dinner on the twenty-fifth. During the day, Arnold received word that a merchant, John Anderson, had been captured. Realizing the game was up, Arnold immediately fled his home, explaining he had business to take care of at the fort. In fact, he went straight to the British.

Washington arrived several hours later at Arnold's home and was surprised that Arnold was not there to greet him. So he decided to inspect the defenses at nearby West Point himself and was disappointed to see the disorganized state of the fort. Arnold had neglected the defenses in preparation for the British takeover. Washington then returned to Arnold's lodgings, where he received shocking news. His aide, Alexander Hamilton, handed him a packet of information that had been found in the boot of a spy, John Anderson. Benedict Arnold was implicated as a traitor.

"Treason of the blackest dye was yesterday discovered," wrote Greene in his general orders of the next day. "General Arnold who commanded at West Point, lost to every sentiment of honor, of public and private obligation, was about to deliver up that important post into the hands of the enemy."[4] When Washington heard the news he nearly broke into tears. Recovering his composure, he sent riders to try to catch Arnold. "Arnold has betrayed us!" he glumly told Hamilton and Lafayette. "Whom can we trust now?"[5]

On October 2, upon Washington's orders, undoubtedly issued as he remembered the fate of Nathan Hale, Major André was hanged as a spy. Benedict Arnold, meanwhile, had successfully crossed to the British lines and was made a brigadier general in the British army.

As the general reflected upon the overall progress of the cause in 1780, he must have been discouraged. Three significant losses had taken place in the south: Howe had received a severe drubbing at Savannah, Lincoln's army was all but completely captured in Charles Town in May, and Gates's army was lost at Camden. One of his chief generals, whom he had recommended for the post at West Point, had betrayed him. His men were again facing a winter with few supplies. Finally, the general he'd chosen to lead the southern campaign, Greene, reported his force of actives was less than eight hundred. Washington again had to reach deep within himself to march on.

The next month Washington moved his army to winter quarters that stretched from West Point to Morristown, where again supplies were in short supply. Continental currency had devalued to such a degree that the saying "not worth a continental" came into use. Congress dithered and the men remained unpaid and unhappy. Not only the troops but also their families suffered for lack of food and clothing. There had been no pay for years and soldiers could send nothing home. On New Year's Day, 1781, the situation passed the murmuring stage and Washington found himself not only fighting a war against the British enemy but also facing rebellion in his own camp.

On that day, the Pennsylvania brigade under General Anthony Wayne mutinied. Two officers who tried to stop them were killed. Over a thousand soldiers gathered and threatened to march on Congress in Philadelphia. They marched to Princeton and opened negotiations. Washington was not unsympathetic to their plight; he, too, was frustrated with a do-nothing Congress, but could not appear to condone a rebellion. "Cross the Delaware with them," he recommended to Wayne, and "draw from them what they consider to be the principal Grievances, and promise to represent faithfully [these grievance] to Congress . . . and endeavor to obtain a redress."[6] The troops refused to cross the river.

In a letter to Greene, Washington recounted that the British had sent two sergeants in civilian attire to negotiate with the rebels, but had no success. In fact, they seemed insulted by the offer. "The Soldiery in General affect to spurn at the idea of turning *Arnolds* (as they express it)," wrote Wayne to Washington.[7] Thus was Benedict Arnold's name ever to be synonymous with traitor. Finally on January 10, 1781, Washington granted amnesty and a release from service to the mostly German immigrant Pennsylvanians. The two British sergeants were hanged.

In May, Washington finally received some good news. A powerful fleet of French ships under the command of Admiral de Grasse had left France and was sailing west. He also learned that Clinton's army in New York was dwindling. On the twenty-second, accompanied by generals Knox and Chevalier Louis Lebegue de Presle de Duportail, Washington met with Rochambeau and Major General François-Jean Beauvoir, chevalier de Chastellux, a French writer and professional soldier. Agreeing that a joint venture between the Americans and French was important, they set about deciding where that should be. As usual, Washington was fixated on New York. Rochambeau concurred. "Upon a full consideration of our affairs," he wrote Lafayette, ". . . an attack upon New York . . . was deemed preferable to a southern operation as we had not the command of the Water."[8] Although Rochambeau posed what-if questions regarding the possibility of de Grasse's fleet arriving soon off Virginia, Washington was unmoved: New York had too long been his goal. But Rochambeau was equally convinced. Unbeknownst to Washington, Rochambeau had advised de Grasse to proceed to Virginia.

The general was also unaware that his letters to Lafayette, detailing his plans to attack New York, had been captured and were in the hands of Clinton. In June, concerned about the impending attack, Clinton ordered Cornwallis—who was in Virginia—to send him three thousand troops. He also recommended to Cornwallis "to take a defensive station in any healthy situation you choose, be it at Williamsburg or Yorktown."[9]After surveying the available sites, Cornwallis chose to establish his main base at the old tobacco-exporting town of Yorktown, which was supported by an additional fort across the York River at Gloucester. By August twenty-second he was in position.

Meanwhile the combined French and American armies now marched for New York, arriving late in July. Their initial observations confirmed what the French admiral already knew: the city was well fortified, the British having had three years to reinforce their positions.

Thus August 14, 1781, was one of the most fateful days in the long war. Washington received a packet of letters from the French admiral Louis Comte de Barras in Newport. In them he learned of de Grasse's departure from the West Indies and that he was sailing to Virginia and not New York. It was also announced that due to weather conditions, the fleet would have to leave America and depart for France in November.

What should Washington do?

In his diary, Washington chronicled his decision. "Matters having now come to a crisis and a decisive plan to be determined on, I was obliged to . . . give up all plans of attacking New York." Instead he would move his troops to Head of Elk, and get transport to Virginia "for the purpose of cooperating with the force from the West Indies against the Troops in that State."[10] His men now needed to march over four hundred miles, and do it quickly. This gut wrenching decision shaped the conduct of the remainder of the war.

August 19 saw the beginning of the march to Yorktown. The troops paraded through Philadelphia to the cheers of the population. Defiantly they paused and demanded a month's pay in hard cash from Congress. Congress got the message and borrowed twenty thousand dollars from the French. The satisfied men received their wages and moved on. After covering nearly two hundred miles in just over two weeks, the army arrived at Head of Elk, Delaware, for transport. There Washington received the intelligence that de Grasse had safely anchored off the coast of the Chesapeake with a fleet consisting of twenty-nine warships and three thousand men.

On September 12 Washington, who had spent four days at Mount Vernon, received a scare: the French fleet had departed. A British fleet, under Admiral Thomas Graves, had appeared off the coast, forcing de Grasse to deal with this threat. Both Cornwallis and Clinton thought Graves could drub the French fleet and remove the threat. They believed the maxim common in that day: one English sailor was worth two French or three Spanish.

They were wrong. De Grasse mangled the British fleet, forcing it back to New York. Comte de Barras had also arrived from Rhode Island, reinforcing the French and bringing siege guns. Cornwallis was now stuck at Yorktown with no way to escape by water. Washington had arrived in Williamsburg, preventing him from leaving the peninsula by land. The noose was tightening and Washington knew it.

"Our Operations here are fast Ripening to the point of their Commencement," he wrote General Robert Howe on September 24. "A Day or two will carry us before the Works of Lord Cornwallis. Our Prospects at present are both fair and promising. What may be in the Womb of Fate is very uncertain; but we anticipate the Reduction of Ld Cornwallis with his Army, with much satisfaction." His army consisted of 7,800 French, 3,100 militia, and 8,000 Continentals. Against him were 9,000 under Cornwallis.[11]

On the twenty-eighth the armies marched to begin the siege of Yorktown. The Americans on the right and the French on the left formed a semicircle measuring about six miles long. Facing them were a series of seven redoubts, or completely enclosed outposts, and six fortified artillery batteries, all linked by entrenchments. Expecting reinforcements and not wanting to spread his men too thin, Cornwallis ordered the evacuation of all but two of these redoubts, numbers 9 and 10, located only a few hundred yards apart.

Yorktown was a small village, maybe sixty houses, but the British were well dug in. Because the French fleet needed to sail by November 1, there was no time to starve out the British. A classic eighteenth-century siege was needed.

The object in a siege is to get the big guns—mortars, howitzers, and cannon—as close as possible to inflict maximum damage. When the walls are breached, infantry can then charge and engage the enemy. To make this happen, a series of trenches, called parallels, are dug in a zigzag manner. The French were masters of this type of warfare, and Washington placed Rochambeau in charge of the siege operations. The diggers, or sappers, are vulnerable to being picked off by rifle fire or bombardment, so to protect them bundles of sticks, called fascines, are made and placed in front of or over them as they dig. The digging began on the evening of October 6, with the general himself breaking ground ceremoniously. The next day two thousand yards had been dug. Two days later the trenches were within six hundred yards of the British and the artillery was ready to fire.

Although his artillery was ready first, Washington deferred to the French, allowing them to begin the bombardment at three o'clock on the afternoon of October 9. They fired with amazing accuracy, not only into the town, but also at several British ships in the York River. As the red-hot cannon balls fell—they were heated in fires first—several ships burst into flames. The rest of the British fleet left the area in fear. Two hours later the Americans opened fire.

"His Excellency, General Washington put the match to the first gun," wrote an observer, "and a furious discharge of cannon and mortars immediately followed."[12] The British responded with their own bombardment, yet they were powerless to stop the advancing sappers. Soon at least forty-six artillery pieces were in range and operating day and night.

By October 14, digging had reached the point that redoubts 9 and 10 had to be taken to continue. These were ringed by *abatis*, felled trees sharpened and pointed at the attacker to slow him down. Past this barrier the British had also placed *fraises*, sharpened sticks firmly planted in the ground pointed toward the attacking forces. The plan was to attack simultaneously and silently just after dark. Number 10, the smaller with just forty-five defenders, was in the American sector. This action was led by Hamilton. The French were led by the Marquis de Deux-Ponts who faced over 120 German and British soldiers.

After a fierce bombardment of the two redoubts, the two led their respective four hundred men to the attack at seven o'clock. Surprise was essential to success. Their muskets were unloaded, to prevent accidental discharge; bayonets only would be used. Only yards from the *abatis* at Redoubt 9, a sentry issued a challenge. The French then charged. Taking the time to hack through the *abatis* impediments, many axemen were silhouetted against the sky and cut down. After a fierce hand-to-hand battle, the rebel forces finally overran the position, forcing the defenders to give up. British losses amounted to 52 dead and 130 wounded.

The Americans suffered fewer casualties. The watchword for the attack was *Rochambeau*, which is pronounced 'Ro-sham-bo.' Private Martin thought it appropriate, for when "pronounced quick, it sounded like *rush on boys*."[13] As the battle began a forlorn hope (suicide) squad of twenty charged. Instead of cutting through the *abatis*, however, they slipped around it. Immediately the rest of the force followed and within minutes the attack was over. Their losses were fifteen killed; one officer, Captain Stephen Olney of Rhode Island, lost part of his intestine to a British bayonet but survived.

With the fall of redoubts 9 and 10 the vice tightened. The allied force now trained one hundred guns on the town of Yorktown, firing day and night. On officer recorded his amazement at the accuracy of the artillery and its damage. "When a shell falls, it whirls round, burrows, and excavates the earth . . . makes dreadful havoc. I have . . . witnessed fragments of the mangled bodies and limbs . . . thrown into the air."[14]

Finally, on the morning of the seventeenth, a British drummer beat the call for a parley. An officer waving a white handkerchief appeared and was led blindfolded into the American–French camp. He carried a letter from Cornwallis to Washington: "Sir, I propose a cessation of hostilities for twenty-four hours," it read, "and that two officers may be appointed by each side, to meet at Mr. Moore's house, to settle terms for the surrender of the posts at York and Gloucester."[15]

"An Ardent Desire to spare the further Effusion of Blood," responded Washington, "will readily incline me to listen to such Terms for the surrender of your Posts and Garrisons."[16]

Initially Cornwallis requested permission for his men to give their parole, return home, and not fight again in the American campaign. "To avoid unnecessary Discussions and Delays," answered an angered Washington, "I shall at Once . . . declare the general Basis upon which a Definitive Treaty and Capitulation must take place." Quickly letting Cornwallis know who was in charge, he declared the parole of the enlisted soldiers was "inadmissible." They were prisoners of war and would be "marched to such parts of the Country as can most conveniently provide for Subsistence." Here Washington could not help but needle his adversary, "and the Benevolent Treatment of Prisoners, which is invariably observed by Americans, will extend to them." These were the same terms that had been forced upon Lincoln at Charles Town.[17]

The two envoys sent by Washington were Colonel John

Laurens, whose father had at one time been president of Congress, and Marquis de Noailles, Lafayette's brother-in-law. They negotiated in the home of a widow Moore until after midnight. On October 19, they reached an agreement. Officers who gave their parole could keep their sidearms and return home; enlisted men would be prisoners for the duration of the war.

At noon, two one hundred–man detachments, one French and one American, stood outside Yorktown and waited for the defeated troops to appear. The rest of the Continental Army on the right and the French on the left lined Hampton Road, stretching half a mile.

Slowly the 7,241 defeated marched between them. Some were sobbing, some defiant, but all were mournful. The colors were furled and cased. "They marched through both armies in a slow pace, and to the sound of music," wrote one observer, "not military marches, but of certain airs which had in them [a] peculiar strain of melancholy."[18] Reputedly, this tune was "The World Turned Upside Down." It was fitting. Because Cornwallis was "sick," he was not among those coming out, so General Charles O'Hara rode at the head.

When he reached the allied officers, O'Hara tried to surrender his sword to Rochambeau, who declined to accept it. He pointed across the road to Washington. Showing "neither irritation nor disappointment," Washington, too, declined and indicated O'Hara should present it to his second in command, General Benjamin Lincoln, who accepted the sword and promptly returned it. The British and German troops then marched to a field, stacked their weapons, and marched into the city of Yorktown.

★ ★ ★

Although the surrender of Cornwallis was a tremendous victory, it did not end the war. The Treaty of Paris, officially ending the conflict, would not be signed until September 3, 1783, nearly two years later. In the meantime, the war continued. Washington sent a large contingent of his men to shore up Greene's forces in Charles Town. After the French fleet sailed away, Rochambeau remained in the Yorktown area. Although the rest of his army wintered in Newburgh, New York, Washington spent his time in Philadelphia. There he continually dealt with a Congress that did not have the power to raise money.

By January 1783, the patience of the unpaid Continental Army was at an end. A petition was sent to Congress asking for back pay, clothing, and provisions. They demanded "just recompense for the several years of hard service, in which the health, and fortunes of the officers have been worn down and exhausted."[19] The threat was implicit. Congress had appealed to the states for funds but those had dried up. Under the Articles of Confederation, the federal government had no power to tax and therefore had to rely on donations from the individual states. February passed with no answer.

Washington had fought this battle almost as long as he had fought the British. Although sympathetic to the officer's petition, he was grounded in civilian authority. "The predicament in which I stand as Citizen and soldier, is as critical and delicate as can well be conceived. It has been the Subject of many contemplative hours," he wrote Hamilton on March 4. "The sufferings of a complaining Army on the one hand, and the inability of Congress and tardiness of the States on the other, are the forebodings of evil." He concluded this letter with what would become his position in the upcoming Constitutional Convention. It was his opinion "Unless Congress have powers competent to all *general* purposes, that the distresses we have encountered, the expence we have incurred, and the blood we have spilt in the course of an Eight year war, will avail us nothing."[20]

On March 10, Washington's fears came to pass. An anonymous officer drafted a document—named the Newburgh Proposals after the location of the main army at Newburgh, New York—threatening to allow the British to retake America or to declare a military coup themselves if their demands were not met. Later that day another pamphlet called for a meeting on March 11. The general orders for that day forbade such a meeting, but Washington rescheduled it for the next Saturday at noon. The future of the army—and perhaps the United States—depended upon what would happen.

At the appointed time on March 15, Washington arrived at the newly constructed building to meet with the unhappy officers. "Visibly agitated," the general walked to the podium. "Gentlemen: By an anonymous summons, an attempt has been made to convene you together," he began. "How inconsistent with the rules of propriety! how unmilitary! and how subversive of all order and discipline."[21]

An emotional and at times angry Washington reminded his officers that "I was among the first who embarked in the cause of our common Country . . . I have never left your side one moment."

The "dreadful alternative" provided in the first pamphlet called for the officers to leave the country if the war continued and let the British decide its fate. Or if peace was made, to stage a coup and thereby receive redress. "My God! what can this writer have in view, by recommending such measures? Can he be a friend to the Army? Can he be a friend to this Country? Rather, is he not an insidious Foe?" Washington demanded. Congress must consider competing demands, he explained, and would certainly, given time, redress their grievances.[22]

Waxing eloquent and passionate in his concluding remarks, he exhorted the officers and appealed to their sense of duty and honor:

> And let me conjure you, in the name of our common Country, as you value your own sacred honor, as you respect the rights of humanity, and as you regard the Military and National character of America, to express your utmost horror and detestation of the Man who wishes . . . to overturn the liberties of our Country . . . and attempt to open the flood Gates of Civil discord, and deluge our rising Empire in Blood . . . And you will, by the dignity of your Conduct, afford occasion for Posterity to say . . . "had this day been wanting, the World had never seen the last stage of perfection to which human nature is capable of attaining."[23]

After completing the speech the officers appeared unmoved. Washington had one last appeal—a letter from Congressman Joseph Jones of Virginia. Unable to make out the small writing, he fumbled for his glasses. "Gentlemen, you must pardon me," he said quietly to the assembly. "I have grown gray in your service and now find myself growing blind." The words brought tears to many in the room. Washington read and then folded the letter, replaced his glasses in his pocket, and walked from the silent room.[24]

After he left, the officers gave him a unanimous vote of confidence, rejected the Newburgh Proposals, and asked the general to continue to mediate for their demands. With this emotional, heartfelt speech, Washington preserved the principal of civilian rule in America and allayed the fears of those who feared a military takeover by a professional standing army. By his example and leadership, he achieved independence for his nation and established military protocols that exist to this day.

Nearly six months later the last British troops departed New York, allowing Washington to return to the city he wanted so badly to free. His only remaining duty was to appear before Congress and resign the commission he had only reluctantly assumed. Then he could finally return to his beloved Martha and the much longed-for life of a gentleman farmer.

Pris de Yorktown: The taking of Yorktown. American, British, and Hessian soldiers fighting.

Surrender of Cornwallis at Yorktown (1797).

SEVENTEEN

Presidency

Of all the dispositions and habits which lead to political prosperity, Religion and morality are indispensable supports.

—GEORGE WASHINGTON

ALTHOUGH WASHINGTON RETIRED from active mili-
tary service, his role in the formation of the fledgling republic had
only begun. Initially he appeared content at resuming the role of
a Virginia plantation owner. "I am become a private citizen on
the banks of the Potomac," he wrote Lafayette in February 1784,
and he was enjoying the solace of being "under the shadow of my
own Vine and my own Fig-tree." For the first time thoughts of
mortality crept into his writings and age began to catch up with
the normally fit and robust general. "I am not only retired from
all public employments," he continued to Lafayette, "but I am

retiring within myself." Pleased with what he saw, his goal was to "move gently down the stream of life, until I sleep with my Fathers." The nation, however, was to make one more demand upon "His Excellency."[1]

Although he may have desired to retire from all "public employments," a grateful and adoring nation of admirers would not allow it. Constant visitors to Mount Vernon, including artists, sculptors, well-wishers, and former colleagues, kept the old general busy and apprised of political events. Increasingly he became concerned with what he saw in the country. The American fear of a standing army caused the military to deteriorate precipitously, even as the British, contrary to the Treaty of Paris, strengthened their presence in the west and armed the increasingly hostile natives. He also viewed with alarm the inability of the federal government to unite and strengthen the union of former colonies. In his view, it was "as plain as any problem in Euclid" and "as clear to me as the A.B.C.," the federal government was too weak to fulfill the needs of the growing republic.[2]

Even as the cause was drawing to a conclusion, Washington was thinking ahead. In June 1783, he composed a "Circular" to each of the thirteen states in which he spelled out his vision for peacetime America. After expounding on the happy events "which Heaven has been pleased to produce in our favor" and his belief that "the foundation of our Empire was not laid in the gloomy age of Ignorance and Superstition, but in an Epocha when the rights of mankind were better understood," he spelled out four essential principles to the "well-being" and even the "existence of the United States as an Independent Power."[3]

Briefly summarized, these principles included "an indissoluble Union of the States under one Federal Head; a sacred regard to Public Justice; adoption of proper Peace Establishment [military forces];" and the "friendly Disposition" of the people to cause them to "forget their local prejudices and policies" and make mutual concessions "to sacrifice their individual advantages to the interests of the Community." Upon these pillars, Washington believed, must rest the national structure.[4]

Just as he had forged a united and successful military out of a motley crew of militia with differing ideas and cultures, Washington would now be called upon to assist in the formation and implementation of a functioning government and bring order to the newly formed union of states. In short, to implement what would become our national motto: *e pluribus unum* (out of many one). The parallels in the two missions are striking. He believed destiny had called him to create an effective unified national military from the weak and disjointed state militia. Likewise his destiny was to bring together thirteen self-centered, independent colonies and attempt to form a consensus government—one that balanced individual liberties with the needs of an overarching federal system. In both endeavors he began from scratch. As in the military, Washington desired to rule with a counsel approach; he strove for consensus and unanimity over absolute authority. To accomplish his task he sought to surround himself with the best minds available. Still, as throughout his military career, his thoughts and concerns were also for his wife and beloved Mount Vernon.

Events came to a head in May 1787, when the Constitutional

Convention convened in Philadelphia to revise the Articles of Confederation. It was quickly apparent, however, that nothing but a complete overhaul of the government would do. Unanimously elected president of the Convention, Washington's role in the formation of the Constitution was critical. Although saying little publicly, his influence was always present. Due to oaths of secrecy, the records of the Convention were not made public until 1819.

As the framers debated what form the Constitution, and thereby the nation, would take, the disagreement over the role and authority of the federal government versus that of the state and local authorities became paramount. In 1786–87, Shays' Rebellion in Massachusetts brought to a head the need for reform. Agrarian farmers, mostly unpaid veterans, saw their land and livelihood lost to wealthy speculators. They rebelled. Closing courts and calling for an overthrow of the existing power structure, they threatened merchants and vowed to create an independent agrarian society. The federal government was powerless to stop them. Shays' Rebellion had a unifying effect upon the supporters of a stronger national government, a lesson frequently cited on the floor of the Federal Convention during deliberations in the summer of 1787. Washington decried the insurrection and gave it as a significant reason for his attendance at the Convention: "there could be no stronger evidence of the want of energy in our governments than these disorders," he declared.[5]

On September 17, 1787, the delegates completed the document, left Philadelphia, and awaited ratification by the states. The process took two years. Although the United States Constitution would not be unanimously ratified until May 1790 (with Rhode

Island's decision), its policies were enacted in June 1789, with the ratification of nine states (New Hampshire being the ninth). As directed by the Constitution, the election of a chief executive took place. Washington, as expected, was unanimously elected president. His inauguration took place May 30, 1789, at Wall Street, New York.

Washington was deeply aware that as the first chief executive, his actions would both establish precedents for future presidents and come under close scrutiny. He, therefore, took pains to act cautiously. Initially refusing to accept the twenty-five thousand-dollar annual salary appropriated by Congress, he soon realized this would limit future participation in politics to the wealthy. Thus he accepted payment. One of his main challenges was not to appear as a monarch or exhibit any royal trappings. Some of these deliberations appear comical to us now. For example, how should Washington be addressed? John Adams, the first vice president, suggested he be referred to as "His Elective Majesty" or "His Mightiness," neither of which appeared suitable to a nation having recently deposed a monarch. (The portly Adams himself was subsequently nicknamed "His Rotundity.") Congress finally settled on "Mr. President."[6]

Chief among Washington's initial challenges was the formation of a group of advisors. Again displaying his gift for selecting talented men and delegating authority to them, he chose James Madison as his main political advisor. The brilliant Madison had written much of the Constitution and, with Washington, composed the Bill of Rights. These ten amendments were added in 1791 to limit federal power and assure civil liberties for individuals. Thomas Jefferson, with his years of dealing with the French, became secretary of state. Alexander Hamilton was chosen as secretary of the treasury. The ever-loyal and competent Henry Knox would also be selected as secretary of defense.

As commander in chief of the military, Washington had sought advice from his trusted generals. The Constitution required the president to seek senatorial "advice and consent." Washington therefore sought to achieve unanimity by counseling with the Senate over several proposed Indian treaties. The result was a disaster. Political wrangling and endless disputes were not in Washington's nature. Another precedent was established. He would make the treaties and then let the Senate deliberate their ratification. Never again would he appear before that body.

Another thorny political problem involved the location of the "seat of government." This residency issue produced a lot of heat but not much light. Historian Joseph J. Ellis reports that "one frustrated congressman suggested sarcastically that perhaps they should put the new capital on wheels and roll it from place to place."[7] Eventually, through negotiations between Hamilton and Madison, the present location along the Potomac River, roughly in the geographic center of the nation, was decided upon. To avoid future division, Washington himself was allowed to work out the details of developing the city. In 1800 the seat of government was moved to what was then renamed the District of Columbia.

As his first term approached an end, the aged general let it be known he did not want to serve a second time, but circumstances, coupled with the belief he was the only man who could unite the nation, caused him to acquiesce. He was again unanimously elected in 1792. His second inaugural address of only four sentences was the shortest in history. "I shall endeavour to express the high sense I entertain of this distinguished honor," he spoke, "and of the confidence that has been reposed in me by the people of United America." He closed by asserting that if he failed to perform his duties, he should be subject to "the upbraidings of all who are now witnesses."[8]

An incident that had its beginnings in 1791 in western Pennsylvania would be the only military challenge awaiting the old general: Congress imposed an excise tax on the distillation of corn liquor. The significance of whiskey in that time cannot be overstated. No gathering of any kind, whether weddings, funerals, barn raisings, even church meetings, took place without libations being served. Water was impure and carbonated beverages had not yet been invented. Taxation was a significant challenge to the producers' profits and the distillers in Pennsylvania decided the federal government did not have the authority to impose such a tax; the government differed. In 1794 Washington himself, as commander in chief, mounted his horse and rode to Carlisle, Pennsylvania, to join the forces arrayed against the insurgents. As the army moved west, the rebels quickly capitulated and no armed confrontation occurred. Thus the principle of federal authority to tax was established.

As the election season of fall 1796 approached, Washington was asked to serve a third term. His refusal set a further precedent, unbroken until 1940 by Franklin Roosevelt, of a two-term limit for the presidency. In his Farewell Address, prepared over the course of nearly two years with the assistance of Madison,

John Jay, and Hamilton, we are treated to not only a brilliant political statement, but also an insight into the character and faith of Washington.

After expressing his appreciation for the honor and trust given to him by the citizenry, Washington reiterated it was time for him to step down. Public officials were servants, not rulers, and selected only for a brief period. In his typically self-deprecating style, he wrote he had contributed "the best exertions of which a very fallible judgment was capable." He was "not unconscious . . . of the inferiority of my qualifications" from the onset.[9]

Concerning domestic policies, the general warned of several dangers and offered his view of political prosperity. The North and South had competing economic and political differences that could split the country. To avoid this, he urged the continuation of "the UNION as a primary object of Patriotic desire." Not only sectionalism challenged the nation but also division into political parties. The existing intransigence between Federalists and Republicans was dangerous and he warned against "the baneful effects of the Spirit of Party, generally." Thus did Washington foresee problems continuing to plague our nation to the present. What could keep us from these perils? "Of all the dispositions and habits which lead to political prosperity," he opined, "Religion and morality are indispensable supports."[10]

Laying the foundation for neutrality, the foundation of our foreign policy until after World War II, he warned the nation "a passionate attachment of one Nation for another produces a variety of evils." This brought the dangers of getting involved in foreign warfare. "The Great rule of conduct for us, in regard to foreign Nations," he believed, "is in extending our commercial relations [and] to have with them as little political connections as possible." The nation must especially be wary of becoming involved in European wars and alliances.[11]

With this address, his excellency, the commander in chief, and president of the United States left his legacy to the American people. Called upon to father both the military and presidency of the United States, Washington was certainly the "Indispensable Man" to perform the task. His leadership abilities, undergirded by his faith and character, and supported by his humility, served to set this nation on the path to greatness.

On Saturday, March 4, 1797, Washington appeared in his last formal official role. The inauguration of John Adams provided an example to the world of how the United States effected the peaceful transition of power. As Adams completed his oath of office, many wept, perhaps as much for the departure of Washington as for the words of Adams. "A solemn scene it was indeed," wrote Adams. He also noted Washington's face "remained as serene and as unclouded as the sky . . . Me thought," continued Adams, "I heard him think, 'Ay! I am fairly out and you are fairly in! See which of us will be the happiest!'"[12]

Legacy

His integrity was most pure . . . this I would vouch at the
judgment seat of God.

—THOMAS JEFFERSON

SINCE HIS DEATH from a combination of infection and
excessive bleeding on December 14, 1799, the life of George
Washington has been an inspiration to countless numbers. He
left not only a political legacy as the first president of the United
States, establishing fine and dignified precedent for future presidents, but a legacy of leadership demonstrated throughout his
military career. History is full of leaders whose egos caused them
to rise quickly in fame and success. Yet like meteors that light
the sky momentarily only to be extinguished, they and their successes are quickly forgotten or undone. Washington's example of

selfless, honorable devotion to duty lives on; his model is both timeless and universal.

Washington was a man of faith. He had confidence in Providence—his preferred term for God—faith in himself, and faith in the future of the nation. This faith undergirded his decisions and actions and was the constant touchstone of his life. He believed and recognized he was a part of something larger than his own ambitions or desires. He understood he had a duty—even a destiny—to fulfill and allowed nothing to turn him from that goal. With singular focus of vision he was able to inspire, motivate, and challenge his followers.

It was his faith in God that allowed him to fearlessly put himself in harm's way during the heat of battle. Time and again, as at the battles of Manhattan and Monmouth, he charged into the thick of it, rallied his troops, and turned what appeared to be defeat into victory.

Fourteen years after Washington's death, Thomas Jefferson, who knew him "intimately and thoroughly," wrote a letter describing Washington's character to a Dr. Walter Jones. He was "incapable of fear, meeting personal dangers with the calmest unconcern." That he always escaped unharmed can only be described as miraculous. The only fear he demonstrated was not that of death, but that his abilities and military experience "may not be equal to the extensive & important Trust" given to him.[1] His formation of the chaplaincy and insistence on providing divine services for the troops consistently reminded them that they and the nascent republic were under "the blessing of heaven," and relied upon "the protection of heaven."[2]

Certainly Washington faced self-doubt. There were times when he was frustrated, fearful, and did not know "what plan of conduct to pursue." On other occasions he lost his temper, with which he struggled mightily, and allowed his emotions free reign. These times were short-lived, however, and his belief in himself and assurance in the rightness of his cause soon restored his confidence and self-control.

The general had a keen and realistic understanding of his men, what motivated them, and how to inspire them at the right time. His ability to train and unite a citizenry as diverse as New England independent farmers, freedmen, Virginia planters, slave holders, merchants, penniless workers, and wealthy gentlemen, into a formidable unified fighting army, and to do so even as he fought a war, is reason enough to call him a great leader. Yet his greatness extended to civilian leadership as well. As president, he held together the two opposing visions of this country—a strong federal government versus state and local authority—as well as individual rights versus the good of the whole. Only Washington could have succeeded in this.

His display of consistent high moral character inspired almost godlike devotion and loyalty among his followers and won the respect even from his enemies. "His integrity was most pure," continued Jefferson; "this I would vouch at the judgment seat of God."[3] His exemplary character and motivational attributes laid the groundwork and provided the template for our modern officer and gentleman corps even as his organizational skills established its underlying framework.

In addition to his faith and character, Washington left a legacy of discipline in the conduct of officers. The success of the military relies upon consistent discipline and obedience to direct, clear orders by motivated and informed troops. Self-discipline was the ideal, yet if men could not or would not control themselves, authority must be exercised. The general did not fear the administration of harsh punishment; lashings and hangings were not infrequent, yet he demanded fairness. His leadership model was to "reward and punish every man according to his merit, without partiality or prejudice." He attempted to be "plain and precise" in his orders lest mistakes or misunderstanding occur. Each soldier "from the first to the lowest" must be motivated by "the rightness of the cause" and what they were fighting for. Men will obey if properly trained, given clear direction, and faithfully led—not driven—by their leaders.[4]

As president his model was the same. He surrounded himself with men he trusted, delegated authority to them, and expected results. Again he led by example. When acting in the role of commander in chief he did not shirk his responsibility but donned his uniform and rode to confront a perceived enemy of his beloved union. Although unsuccessful, since the military was basically dismantled after the Revolution, he strove to create, maintain, and develop a professional national military force. His principles remained the core of the future military establishment.

When on December 23, 1783, the general appeared before Congress—the highest civilian authority in America—and, like the ancient Roman dictator Cincinnatus, surrendered his sword and commission, he demonstrated he both understood and exemplified the principle of being a man under authority. Despite its constant failings, divisions, and incompetence throughout the war, Washington had submitted himself to congressional authority. In so doing he established the principle of civilian control over the military. Unlike many other nations, the United States has never seriously feared a military coup—since Washington. Had he desired, the mood in the country was such he probably could have pronounced himself dictator, or at least have won a third term as president. Our history, however, has demonstrated notable examples of chief executives who have disciplined senior officers for breaches of etiquette or disobedience to orders. This is Washington's gift to his nation.[5]

Perhaps Jefferson leaves us with the best eulogy for Washington: "He was indeed in every sense of the word, a wise, a good, and a great man." Jefferson concluded his letter to Jones, "I felt on his death, with my countrymen, that, Verily a great man hath fallen this day in the house of Israel."[6]

Notes

PROLOGUE

1. Freeman, *George Washington: A Biography*, 5:473.

2. Ibid., 5:474. At his death Washington probably had only one natural tooth in his head. He did not, however, have wooden teeth. Like others of his day, his false teeth would have been made of ivory, bone, or even teeth pulled from the mouths of healthy slaves. We have no pictures of him smiling because the spring that opened and closed the dentures was difficult to control and his "dentures" could slip. A more detailed description is included in the National Geographic video *The Real George Washington*, available online.

3. Ibid., 5:475–6.

4. Ibid.

5. Ibid., 5:476–7.

6. Ibid., 5:477.

7. "Eulogy of George Washington," http://gwpapers.virginia.edu/project/exhibit/mourning/response.html (accessed November 9, 2010).

8. Thompson, *Hands of a Good Providence*. Among those arguing that Washington was a Deist include Boller's classic *George Washington and Religion*. Boller's thesis that "George Washington appears as a Deist, not a devout Christian" (p. 28) is refuted in Lillback's *George Washington's Sacred Fire*, and Novak's *Washington's God*. Basically the standards of a professing Anglican in Virginia during the late-eighteenth-century include "baptism, acceptance of the Apostles' and Nicene Creeds . . . and some regular attendance at church . . . It seems quite clear that Washington easily met the standards for being considered an Anglican in good standing," 212.

INTRODUCTION

1. Freeman, *Washington*, introduction by Michael Kammen (New York: Touchstone, 1995), xvii. In a March 1953 radio interview, found in Kammen's introduction, Freeman expressed his views on Weems's book: "Weems was absurdly in error with respect to detail; [but] he was fundamentally correct in his interpretation of the man." Later after explaining how some have tried to debunk Washington as hero, he concluded, "I think that Parson Weems was far more nearly accurate in his appraisal than the debunkers have been."

2. Fitzpatrick, "December 23, 1788," *Writings of George Washington, Vol. 30* (Washington, DC: U.S. Government Printing Office, 1939).

3. Quoted in Lillback, *George Washington's Sacred Fire*, 99.

4. Ibid.

5. A listing of the "Rules of Civility" found at http://www.history.org./almanack/life/manners/rules2.cfm (accessed November 11, 2010).

6. Quoted in Lillback, *George Washington's Sacred Fire*, 983.

7. Jackson and Twohig, *Diaries: 1748-1765*, 1:6-23. A note about Washington's spelling and grammar. I have tried to maintain both the original language and often misspellings. At this time there were no hard and fast rules. As in German, most nouns were capitalized.

8. Ibid., 1:33.

CHAPTER ONE

1. Flexner, *The Forge of Experience*, 191-2.

2. Jackson and Twohig, *Diaries, 1748-1765*, 1:126-28. Lawrence had also been an officer in the Ohio Company, thus having a financial stake in its success.

3. Ibid., 1:130.

4. Ibid., 1:132.

5. Ibid., 1:133, 135.

6. Ibid., 1:136-37.

7. Ibid., 1:144.

8. Ibid., 1:147.

9. Ibid., 1:148-49.

10. Ibid., 1:152.

11. Ibid., 1:154-56. Parts of Gist's diary are included in this edition of Washington's Diaries.

12. Ibid., 1:157.

13. Ibid., 1:155.

14. Ibid., 1:158-60.

CHAPTER TWO

1. Jackson and Twohig, *Diaries, 1748–1765*, 1:151, n. 59.

2. Ibid., 1:160–61.

3. Ibid., 1:126.

4. Ibid., 1:164.

5. Fitzpatrick, "March 9, 1754," *Writings of George Washington, Vol. 1*.

6. Jackson and Twohig, *Diaries, 1748–1765*, 1:65.

7. Ibid., 1:88.

8. Anderson, Fred, *Crucible of War*, 48–49.

9. Abbot, *Papers of George Washington, Colonial series*, 1:105

10. Ibid., 1:195.

11. Jackson and Twohig, *Diaries, 1748–1765*, 1:195.

12. Abbot, *Papers of George Washington, Colonial Series*, 1:118–19.

13. Jackson and Twohig, *Diaries, 1748–1765*, 1:199.

14. Anderson, *Crucible of War*, 60.

15. Ibid., 61.

16. Quoted in Anderson, *Crucible of War*, 61.

17. Abbot, *Papers of George Washington, Colonial Series*, 1:160.

18. Anderson, *Crucible of War*, 64.

19. Abbot, *Papers of George Washington, Colonial Series*, 1:165-6.

20. Ibid., 1:209; see also Axelrod, *Blooding at Great Meadows*, 241-2.

21. Abbot, *Papers of George Washington, Colonial Series*, 1:224.

22. Axelrod, *Blooding at Great Meadows*, 244.

23. Accounts differ of the events of the battle and de Jumonville's death. According to Jackson and Twohig (*Diaries*, 1:114), a Canadian eyewitness named Monceau claimed the French were on a peaceful diplomatic mission to order Washington to leave the French area, much like Washington's previous expedition. Monceau fled when the battle commenced; de Jumonville was still alive. An Indian who was present gave an account of how de Jumonville died. He stated the English had killed de Jumonville in cold blood before he could make his intentions known; this man claimed only the intervention of the Indians had saved the rest of the French from annihilation.

Two other accounts of the incident soon surfaced. One came from a deserter named Denis Kaninguen, a member of Washington's camp. His account—given to the French and forwarded to Montreal—stated that de Jumonville was wounded in the initial attack by Washington and then killed by Tanacharison with several hatchet blows. Kaninguen then noted the French prisoners were taken to Virginia where he escaped and went to the French.

A third story was told by Private John Shaw. Although not present, Shaw had heard from many who were. He maintained that the French were just getting up in the morning, found themselves surrounded by Washington, and fired upon him. The English then returned fire, scattering the French; however, their route was blocked by the Indian contingent, so they surrendered to Washington. Half King, who had personal reasons to hate the French, attacked the wounded de Jumonville while he was being interrogated, bashing his skull and "washing" his hands in the brains. The other Indians present killed and scalped the remainder of the French wounded and took their weapons.

CHAPTER THREE

1. Abbott, *Papers of George Washington, Colonial Series*, 1:232–234.

2. Ibid., 1:241–2.

3. Ibid., 1:243.

4. These are named after Baron Menno van Coehoorn, who, in the late seventeenth century, developed a portable mortar. Mortars are shaped like the pharmacist's tool from which they get their name. Howitzers are short cannon, firing a heavy shell, with a lower trajectory than a mortar. Cannon were described by the weight of the shell they fired, for example, a four-pounder fired a four-pound shell. (Abbot, *Papers of George Washington, Colonial Series*, 1:327.)

5. Ibid., 1:271.

6. Anderson, *Crucible of War*, 95–6.

7. Washington revised his letter book of the Braddock campaign several times, the first probably no earlier than the 1770s. I have used the original writing when possible. I have only corrected spelling where appropriate and when the meaning is not affected. Where there are erasures or illegible entries I have indicated these by the encompassing them with the symbols [and closing]. For a complete discussion of the editing of Washington's writings see Abbott, *Papers of George Washington, Colonial Series*, 1:237–242.

8. Ibid., 1:343.

9. Ibid., 1:341, n. 7. Describes how subsequently a medical examination of the bodies found the presence of the larger British balls, many in the back, leading to the conclusion friendly fire was responsible for the majority of deaths.

10. Ibid., 1:336.

11. Ibid., 1:333, n. 4.

12. Ibid., 1:339.

13. Ibid., 1:343.

14. Ibid., 1:350.

15. Federer, *Encyclopedia of Quotations*, 636–7; and Lossing, *Pictorial Field-Book of the Revolution: Vol. 2*.

16. Lillback, *George Washington's Sacred Fire*, 999.

17. Abbot, *Papers of George Washington, Colonial Series*, 1:359.

18. Ibid., 1:361.

19. Ibid., 1:361–3.

20. Abbot, *Papers of George Washington, Colonial Series*, 2:257.

21. Ibid.

22. Abbot, *Papers of George Washington, Colonial Series*, 5:102–6.

23. Flexner, *The Forge of Experience*, 192.

CHAPTER FOUR

1. Fitzpatrick, "September 1, 1758," *Writings of George Washington*, 2:262.

2. Ibid., 2:277.

3. Ibid., 2:275.

4. Novak, *Washington's God*, 59.

5. Anderson, *Crucible of War*, 280–3.

6. Fitzpatrick, *Writings of George Washington*, 2:425–6.

7. Fitzpatrick, "April 5, 1759," *Writings of George Washington*, 2:501–4.

8. Boatner, *Encyclopedia of the American Revolution*, 624–31.

9. Fitzpatrick, "To George Fairfax, May 31, 1775," *Writings of George Washington*, 3:292.

10. Chase, *Papers of George Washington, Revolutionary War Series*, 1:2.

11. Ibid., 1:1.

12. Ibid., 1:4.

13. Ibid., 1:14.

CHAPTER FIVE

1. Chase, *Papers of George Washington, Revolutionary War Series*, 1:92.

2. Ibid., 1:27.

3. Ibid., 1:135.

4. Fitzpatrick, "July 4, 1775," *Writings of George Washington*, 3:308–9.

5. Ibid., 3:309.

6. Ibid., 3:448.

7. Ibid., 4:80–1.

8. Ibid., 3:309–10.

9. Ibid., 3:440.

10. Ibid., 3:450.

11. Thacher, *Military Journal*, 32.

12. Ibid., 32–3.

13. Hogan and Taylor, *My Dearest Friend*, 59.

14. Wood, *Battles of the Revolutionary War*, xxii–xxxii.

15. Chase, *Papers of George Washington, Revolutionary War Series*, 3:88.

16. Ibid., 2:449.

17. Ibid., 3:89.

18. Ibid., 3:1.

19. Ibid., 3:1–3.

20. Ibid.

21. Ibid., 3:179–80.

22. Thacher, *Military Journal*, 41.

23. Hogan and Taylor, *My Dearest Friend*, 99.

24. Thacher, *Military Journal*, 43.

25. Chase, *Papers of George Washington, Revolutionary War Series*, 3:569.

26. Hogan and Taylor, *My Dearest Friend*, 105.

27. Chase, *Papers of George Washington, Revolutionary War Series*, 2:244.

CHAPTER SIX

1. Lengel, *A Military Life*, 132.

2. Schecter, *Battle for New York*, 3–5.

3. Chase, *Papers of George Washington, Revolutionary War Series*, 3:20.

4. Ibid., 4:67.

5. Ibid., 4:412–14.

6. Ibid.

7. Ibid., 5:130.

8. Showman, Cobb, and McCarthy, *Papers of General Nathanael Greene*, 1:219.

9. Schecter, *Battle for New York*, 117–18.

10. Chase, *Papers of George Washington, Revolutionary War Series*, 5:180.

11. Ibid., 5:180–1.

12. Ibid., 5:219.

13. Ibid., 5:258.

14. Ibid., 5:246.

15. Ibid., 5:256–7.

16. Ibid., 5:296; see also Schecter, *Battle for New York*, 100, for Howe's motives.

17. Chase, *Papers of George Washington, Revolutionary War Series*, 5:306–8, 5:96–7; see also Carbone, *Washington: Lessons in Leadership*, 81.

18. Chase, *Papers of George Washington, Revolutionary War Series*, 5:308.

19. Ibid., 5:399–402. This is recounted in Ellis, *His Excellency George Washington*, 94.

20. Chase, *Papers of George Washington, Revolutionary War Series*, 5:682.

CHAPTER SEVEN

1. Scheer and Rankin, *Rebels and Redcoats*, 160.

2. Field, *Battle of Long Island*, 351.

3. Schecter, *Battle for New York*, 113.

4. Showman, Cobb, and McCarthy, *Papers of General Nathanael Greene*, 1:292.

5. Chase, *Papers of George Washington, Revolutionary War Series*, 5:21.

6. Chase and Grizzard Jr., *Papers of George Washington, Revolutionary War Series*, 6:109–10.

7. Ibid., 6:128.

8. Ibid.

9. Martin, *Narrative of a Revolutionary Soldier*, 24.

10. Ibid., 22, 25.

11. Schecter, *Battle for New York*, 157; also quoted in Graydon, *Memoirs of His Own Time*, Little, ed., 147.

12. Scheer and Rankin, *Rebels and Redcoats*, 171.

13. Martin, *Narrative of a Revolutionary Soldier*, 26.

14. Chase and Grizzard, *Papers of George Washington, Revolutionary War Series*, 6:199.

15. Ibid.

16. Showman, Cobb, and McCarthy, *Papers of General Nathanael Greene*, 1:296.

17. Martin, *Narrative of a Revolutionary Soldier*, 30.

18. Chase and Grizzard, *Papers of George Washington, Revolutionary War Series*, 6:313.

19. Quoted in Carbone, *Lessons in Leadership*, 93.

20. Schecter, *Battle for New York*, 186.

21. Chase and Grizzard, *Papers of George Washington, Revolutionary War Series*, 6:442.

22. Ibid., 6:393–401.

CHAPTER EIGHT

1. Lengel, *General George Washington*, 158.

2. Martin, *Narrative of a Revolutionary Soldier*, 37–8. The green-clad Hessian *Jaegers* (hunters) were originally recruited from gamekeepers and foresters; used as light infantry, they were expert marksmen. The French equivalent was called *chasseurs* (Boatner, *Encyclopedia*, 549).

3. Schecter, *Battle for New York*, 204–209.

4. Quoted in Rose, *Washington's Spies*, 31–2.

5. Quoted in McCullough, *1776*, 232.

6. Chase, *Papers of George Washington, Revolutionary War Series*, 7:115–16.

7. Ibid., 7:162.

8. Ibid., 7:103.

9. Ibid., 7:187.

10. Ibid., 7:237–8.

11. Ibid., 7:238.

12. Whigs and Tories became part of the British political lexicon around 1650. Both terms originally had derogatory connotations. "Whigs" derived from *whiggamore*, a Scottish insurgent, and "Tory" applied to an Irish outlaw. By 1776, Whigs were associated with politics supporting the colonies. Tories were those who supported royal authority (Boatner, *Encyclopedia*, 1197).

13. Quoted in Fischer, *Washington's Crossing*, 125.

14. Fitzpatrick, "To Lee: Dec. 10, 1776," *The Writings of George Washington, Vol. 6.*

15. Fitzpatrick, "Dec. 14, 1776," *The Writings of George Washington, Vol. 6.*

16. Carbone, *Lessons in Leadership*, 108.

17. Chase, *Papers of George Washington, Revolutionary War Series*, 7:336.

18. Quoted in Fischer, *Washington's Crossing*, 133.

CHAPTER NINE

1. Chase, *Papers of George Washington, Revolutionary War Series*, 7:245.

2. Ibid., 7:314; 7:310.

3. Ibid., 7:328.

4. Ibid., 7:365.

5. Ibid., 7:370.

6. Quoted in Slaughter, *Common Sense and Related Writings*, 126.

7. Ibid., 128–9.

8. Quoted in McCullough, *1776*, 269.

9. Chase, *Papers of George Washington, Revolutionary War Series*, 7:415.

10. Ketchum, *Winter Soldiers*, 240–1.

11. Stryker, *Battles of Trenton and Princeton*, 361.

12. Chase, *Papers of George Washington, Revolutionary War Series*, 7:423.

13. Boatner, *Encyclopedia*, 342.

14. Stryker, *Battles of Trenton and Princeton*, 361.

15. Ibid., 362.

16. Quoted in Chase, *Papers of George Washington, Revolutionary War Series*, 7:457.

17. Ibid., 7:454.

18. Boatner, *Encyclopedia*, 1114–5.

19. Chase, *Papers of George Washington, Revolutionary War Series*, 7:458.
20. Ibid., 7:454.
21. Ibid., 7:458–9.
22. Stryker, *Battles of Trenton and Princeton*, 364.
23. Chase, *Papers of George Washington, Revolutionary War Series*, 7:456.

CHAPTER TEN

1. Quoted in Fischer, *Washington's Crossing*, 259.
2. Chase, *Papers of George Washington, Revolutionary War Series*, 7:456.
3. Ibid., 7:449.
4. Scheer and Rankin, *Rebels and Redcoats*, 216.
5. Ibid.
6. Chase, *Papers of George Washington, Revolutionary War Series*, 7:462.
7. Stryker, *Battles of Trenton and Princeton*, 244.
8. Chase, *Papers of George Washington, Revolutionary War Series*, 7:500.
9. Ibid., 7:510.
10. Quoted in Fischer, *Washington's Crossing*, 305.
11. Ibid., 306–7.
12. Wood, *Battles of the Revolutionary War*, 79.
13. Chase, *Papers of George Washington, Revolutionary War Series*, 7:526.
14. Ketchum, *Winter Soldiers*, 308.
15. Scheer and Rankin, *Rebels and Redcoats*, 219.
16. Lengel, *General George Washington*, 206–7.
17. Chase, *Papers of George Washington, Revolutionary War Series*, 7:523.
18. Ibid.

CHAPTER ELEVEN

1. Chase, *Papers of George Washington, Revolutionary War Series*, 8:455, 459.
2. Ibid., 8:455
3 Ibid., 9:140.
4. Grizzard, *Papers of George Washington, Revolutionary War Series*, 8:453–4.
5. Ibid., 8:382, 456, 643.
6. Lengel, *General George Washington*, 221.
7. Chase and Lengel, *Papers of George Washington, Revolutionary War Series*, 11:49–51.
8. Chase, *Papers of George Washington, Revolutionary War Series*, 9:49–51.
9. Wood, *Battles of the Revolutionary War*, 99.
10. Ibid., 100.
11. Ibid., 108.

12. Ibid., 110.

13. Scheer and Rankin, *Rebels and Redcoats*, 237.

14. Quoted in Lengel, *General George Washington*, 242.

CHAPTER TWELVE

1. Chase and Lengel, *Papers of George Washington, Revolutionary War Series*, 11:210.

2. Ibid., 11:211–12.

3. Ibid., 11:301–2, 416–418.

4. Ibid., 11:301–2.

5. Ibid., 11:302.

6. Ibid., 11:373–4.

7. Ibid.

8. Lengel, *General George Washington*, 255.

9. Boatner, *Encyclopedia of the American Revolution*, 429.

10. Martin, *Narrative of a Revolutionary Soldier*, 64.

11. Grizzard and Hoth, *Papers of George Washington, Revolutionary War Series*, 12:26.

CHAPTER THIRTEEN

1. Scheer and Rankin, *Rebels and Redcoats*, 289.

2. Chase and Lengel, *Papers of George Washington, Revolutionary War Series*, 11:427.

3. Grizzard and Hoth, *Papers of George Washington, Revolutionary War Series*, 12:620.

4. Ibid., 12:613; see also Boatner, *Encyclopedia*, 1137.

5. Scheer and Rankin, *Rebels and Redcoats*, 291.

6. Grizzard and Hoth, *Papers of George Washington, Revolutionary War Series*, 12:683–7.

7. Ibid.

8. Lengel, *Papers of George Washington, Revolutionary War Series*, 13:7.

9. Ibid., 13:514.

10. Federer, *Encyclopedia of Quotations*, 823.

11. Lengel, *Papers of George Washington, Revolutionary War Series*, 13:505–6.

12. Ibid., 13:30.

13. Ibid., 13:377–8.

14. Ibid., 13:376–404.

15. Ibid., 13:610.

16. Ibid., 13:366.

17. Ibid., 13:68.

18. Showman, McCarthy, and Cobb, *Papers of General Nathanael Greene*, 2:260.

19. Ibid.

20. Grizzard and Hoth, *Papers of George Washington, Revolutionary War Series*, 12:111, 129–30.

21. Showman, McCarthy, and Cobb, *Papers of General Nathanael Greene*, 2:260–1.

22. Lengel, *Papers of George Washington, Revolutionary War Series*, 13:119.

23. Lengel, *General George Washington*, 282.

24. Lengel, *Papers of George Washington, Revolutionary War Series*, 15:38–40.

25. Ibid.

CHAPTER FOURTEEN

1. Lengel, *Papers of George Washington, Revolutionary War Series*, 15:152.

2. Scheer and Rankin, *Rebels and Redcoats*, 326.

3. Lengel, *Papers of George Washington, Revolutionary War Series*, 15:322–3.

4. Ibid., 15:521, 526; see also Showman, McCarthy, Margaret Cobb, *Papers of General Nathanael Greene*, 2:447.

5. Lengel, *Papers of George Washington, Revolutionary War Series*, 15:541–2.

6. Lengel, *General George Washington*, 300.

7. Showman, McCarthy, and Cobb, *Papers of General Nathanael Greene*, 2:450–51.

8. Chernow, *Alexander Hamilton*, 114–115.

9. Martin, *Narrative of a Revolutionary Soldier*, missing page.

10. Lengel, *Papers of George Washington, Revolutionary War Series*, 15:583–4.

11. Ibid., 15:594–5.

12. Ibid., 15:595–6.

CHAPTER FIFTEEN

1. Hoth, *Papers of George Washington, Revolutionary War Series*, 16:15, 20.

2. Ibid., 16:387–90.

3. Ibid.

4. Quoted in Ketchum, *Winter Soldiers*, 26.

5. Chase, *Papers of George Washington, Revolutionary War Series*, 2:125.

6. Ibid., 2:354.

7. Ibid., 2:611.

8. Lengel, *Papers of George Washington, Revolutionary War Series*, 13:125.

9. Showman, McCarthy, and Cobb, *Papers of General Nathanael Greene*, 2:466.

10. Hoth, *Papers of George Washington, Revolutionary War Series*, 16:397.

11. Ibid., 16:370–72.

12. Quoted in Lengel, *General George Washington*, 308.

13. Hoth, *Papers of George Washington, Revolutionary War Series*, 16:459.

14. Lengel, *General George Washington*, 311–12.

15. Carbone, *Nathanael Greene*, 123–4.

16. Martin, *Narrative of a Revolutionary Soldier*, 148.

17. Fitzpatrick, "January 8, 1780," *Writings of George Washington*, 17:362–3.

18. Ibid., 17:449–50.

CHAPTER SIXTEEN

1. Quoted in Carbone, *Lessons in Leadership*, 167.

2. Fitzpatrick, "To Rochambeau, September 8, 1780," *Writings of George Washington*, 20:170.

3. Scheer and Rankin, *Rebels and Redcoats*, 378.

4. Ibid., 384.

5. Chernow, *Alexander Hamilton*, 141.

6. Fitzpatrick, "January 3–4, 1781 to Brigadier General Anthony Wayne," *The Writings of George Washington*, 21:56–7.

7. Ibid., 21:88.

8. Ibid., 22:143.

9. Boatner, *Encyclopedia*, 1234.

10. Jackson and Twohig, *Diaries of George Washington*, 3:410.

11. Fitzpatrick, "September 24, 1781 to Major General Robert Howe," *Writings of George Washington*, 23:132.

12. Thacher, *Military Journal*, 274.

13. Martin, *Narrative of a Revolutionary Soldier*, 202.

14. Thacher, *Military Journal*, 275.

15. Freeman, *George Washington*, 5:377.

16. Fitzpatrick, *Writings of George Washington*, 23:236.

17. Ibid., 23:237.

18. Freeman, *George Washington*, 5:388, n. 47. For a discussion of this issue see http://www.colonialmusic.org/Resource/Schrader.htm.

19. Lengel, *General George Washington*, 346.

20. Fitzpatrick, "March 15, 1783, to the Officers of the Army," *Writings of George Washington*, 26:222–27.

21. Ibid., 26:222–23.

22. Ibid., 26:224–25.

23. Ibid., 26:227.

24. Ibid., 26:222.

CHAPTER SEVENTEEN

1. Commins, "To Marquis de Lafayette, February 1, 1784," *Basic Writings of George Washington*, 507–8.

2. Ellis, *His Excellency: George Washington*, 150.

3. Commins, *Basic Writings of George Washington*, 488–89.

4. Ibid., 491.

5. Calliope Film Resources, "Shays' Rebellion," copyright 2000 CFR, www.calliope.org/shays/shays2.html (accessed October 13, 2010).

6. Ellis, *His Excellency*, 193.

7. Ibid., 206.

8. Commins, *Basic Writings of George Washington*, 597–98.

9. Ibid., 627–29.

10. Ibid., 631–37.

11. Ibid., 637–41.

12. McCullough, *John Adams*, 469.

EPILOGUE

1. Parker, *Letters and Addresses of Thomas Jefferson*, 235.

2. Chase, *Papers of George Washington, Revolutionary War Series*, 5:246.

3. Ibid., 5:235–238.

4. Ibid., 1:346–47.

5. Lucius Quinctius Cincinnatus was a fifth-century BC farmer who left his land to briefly become dictator of Rome. He personally led the Roman infantry into battle. After defeating Rome's enemies, Cincinnatus voluntarily gave up his power and returned to his plow.

6. Parker, *Letters and Addresses of Thomas Jefferson*, 238.

Bibliography

Anderson, Fred. *Crucible of War: The Seven Years' War and the Fate of Empire in British North America, 1754–1766.* New York: Alfred Knopf, 2000; New York: Vintage Press, 2001.

———. "The Hinge of the Revolution: George Washington Confronts a People's Army, July 3, 1775." *Massachusetts Historical Review 1*, 1999.

Axelrod, Alan. *Blooding at Great Meadows: Young George Washington and the Battle that Shaped the Man.* Philadelphia: Running Press Book Publishers, 2007.

Barton, David. *The Bulletproof George Washington.* Texas: Wallbuilder Press, 2003.

Boatner, Mark Mayo. *Encyclopedia of the American Revolution.* New York: St. Martin's Press, 1991.

Boller, Paul F. Jr. *George Washington and Religion.* Dallas: Southern Methodist University Press, 1963.

Calliope Film Resources. "Shays' Rebellion." copyright 2000 CFR. www.calliope.org/shays/shays2.html (accessed 13 October 2010).

Carbone, Gerald M. *Washington: Lessons in Leadership.* New York: Palgrave Macmillan, 2009.

———. *Nathanael Greene: A Biography of the American Revolution.* New York: Palgrave Macmillan, 2008.

Chernow, Ron. *Alexander Hamilton.* New York: Penguin Press, 2004.

Commins, Saxe, ed. *Basic Writings of George Washington.* New York: Random House, 1948.

Ellis, Joseph J. *His Excellency: George Washington.* New York: Vintage Books, 2005.

Ewald, Johann. *Diary of the American War: A Hessian Journal.* Translated and edited by Joseph P. Tustin. New Haven: Yale University Press, 1979.

Federer, William J. *America's God and Country: Encyclopedia of Quotations.* St. Louis: Fame Publishing, 1996.

Field, Thomas W. *Battle of Long Island.* Brooklyn: Long Island Historical Society, 1869.

239

Fischer, David Hackett. *Washington's Crossing*. New York: Oxford University Press, 2004.

Flexner, James Thomas. *George Washington: The Forge of Experience (1732–1775)*. Boston: Little, Brown, 1965.

Freeman, Douglas Southall. *George Washington: A Biography—Victory with the Help of France*, Vol. 5. New York: Charles Scribner's Sons, 1952.

———. *Washington*. Richard Harwell, ed. New York: Charles Scribner's Sons, 1968.

Graydon, Alexander. *Memoirs of His Own Time*. John Stockton Little, ed. Philadelphia: Lindsay & Blakiston, 1846.

Hogan, Margaret A., and C. James Taylor, eds. *My Dearest Friend, Letters of Abigail and John Adams*. Cambridge: Belknap Press of Harvard University Press, 2007.

Ketchum, Richard M. *Winter Soldiers: The Battles for Trenton and Princeton*. New York: Henry Holt, 1999.

———. *Divided Loyalties: How the American Revolution Came to New York*. New York: Henry Holt, 2002.

———. *Victory at Yorktown: The Campaign That Won the Revolution*. New York: Henry Holt, 2004.

Lengel, Edward G. *General George Washington: A Military Life*. New York: Random House Publishing, 2005.

Lillback, Peter. *George Washington's Sacred Fire*. Bryn Mawr, PA: Providence Forum Press, 2006.

Lossing, Benson J. *The Pictorial Field-Book of the Revolution: Vol. 2*. Rutland, VT: Tuttle Co., 1972. Originally published in 1859.

Mackenzie, Frederick. *Diary of Frederick Mackenzie*. Cambridge, MA: Harvard University Press, 1930.

Martin, Joseph Plumb. *A Narrative of a Revolutionary Soldier*. New York: Signet Classic, 2001. Originally published in 1830.

Maynard, C. *A Nelson Companion: A Guide to the Royal Navy of Jack Aubrey*. London: Michael O' Mara Books, 2003.

McCullough, David. *1776*. London: Allen Lane Publishing, 2005.

———. *John Adams*. New York: Simon and Schuster, 2001.

Nelson, James L. *George Washington's Great Gamble and the Sea Battle that Won the American Revolution*. New York: McGraw-Hill, 2010.

Novak, Michael, and Jana Novak. *Washington's God: Religion, Liberty, and the Father of Our Country*. New York: Basic Books, 2006.

Parker, William B., ed. *Letters and Addresses of Thomas Jefferson*. New York: A. Wessels Co., 1907.

Rose, Alexander. *Washington's Spies: The Story of America's First Spy Ring*. New York: Bantam Books, 2007.

Schecter, Barnet. *The Battle for New York: The City at the Heart of the American Revolution*. New York: Walker, 2002.

Scheer, George F., and Hugh Rankin. *Rebels and Redcoats*. Cleveland: World Publishing, 1957.

Slaughter, Thomas, ed. *Thomas Paine: Common Sense and Related Writings*. Boston: Bedford/St. Martin's, 2001.

Stryker, William S. *The Battles of Trenton & Princeton*. Spartanburg, SC: Reprint Co., 1967. Originally published in 1898.

———. *The Battle of Monmouth*. Princeton: Princeton University Press, 1927.

Thacher, James. *A Military Journal During the American Revolutionary War*. Boston: Richardson and Lord, 1823.

Thompson, Mary V. *In the Hands of a Good Providence: Religion in the Life of George Washington*. Charlottesville: University of Virginia Press, 2008.

Wood, W. J. *Battles of the Revolutionary War 1775–1781*. New York: Da Capo Press, 1995.

THE PAPERS OF GEORGE WASHINGTON, DIARIES

Jackson, Donald, and Dorothy Twohig, eds. *The Diaries of George Washington: 1748–1765*. Charlottesville: University Press of Virginia, 1976.

———. *The Diaries of George Washington: 1771–1775, 1780–1781*. Charlottesville: University Press of Virginia, 1978.

THE PAPERS OF GEORGE WASHINGTON, COLONIAL SERIES (10 VOLUMES)

Abbott, W. W., ed., *The Papers of George Washington, Colonial Series, 1748–August 1755*. Vol. 1. Charlottesville: University of Virginia Press, 1983.

———. *The Papers of George Washington, Colonial Series, August 1755–April 1756*, Vol. 2. Charlottesville: University of Virginia Press, 1983.

———. *The Papers of George Washington, Colonial Series, October 1757–September 1758*. Vol. 5. Charlottesville: University of Virginia Press, 1988.

Abbot, W. W., and Dorothy Twohig, eds. *The Papers of George Washington, Colonial Series, January 1761–June 1767*. Vol. 7. Charlottesville: University of Virginia Press, 1990.

THE PAPERS OF GEORGE WASHINGTON, REVOLUTIONARY WAR SERIES (16 VOLUMES)

Chase, Philander D., ed. *The Papers of George Washington, Revolutionary War Series, June–September 1775*. Vol. 1. Charlottesville: University of Virginia Press, 1985.

———. *The Papers of George Washington, Revolutionary War Series, September–December 1775*. Vol. 2. Charlottesville: University of Virginia Press, 1987.

———. *The Papers of George Washington, Revolutionary War Series, January–March 1776*. Vol. 3. Charlottesville: University of Virginia Press, 1988.

———. *The Papers of George Washington, Revolutionary War Series, April–June 1776*. Vol. 4. Charlottesville: University of Virginia Press, 1991.

———. *The Papers of George Washington, Revolutionary War Series, June–August 1776*. Vol. 5. Charlottesville: University of Virginia Press, 1993.

Chase, Philander D., and Frank E. Grizzard Jr., eds. *The Papers of George Washington, Revolutionary War Series, August–October 1776*. Vol. 6. Charlottesville: University of Virginia Press, 1994.

Chase, Philander D., ed. *The Papers of George Washington, Revolutionary War Series, October 1776–January 1777*. Vol. 7. Charlottesville: University of Virginia Press, 1997. Vol. 7.

Grizzard, Frank E. Jr., ed. *The Papers of George Washington, Revolutionary War Series, January–April 1777.* Vol. 8. Charlottesville: University of Virginia Press, 1998.

Chase, Philander D., ed. *The Papers of George Washington, Revolutionary War Series, April–June 1777.* Vol. 9. Charlottesville: University of Virginia Press, 1999.

Chase, Philander D., and Edward G. Lengel, eds. *The Papers of George Washington, Revolutionary War Series, August–October 1777.* Vol. 11. Charlottesville: University of Virginia Press, 2001.

Grizzard, Frank E. Jr., and David R. Hoth, eds. *The Papers of George Washington, Revolutionary War Series, October–December 1777.* Charlottesville: University of Virginia Press, 2002. Vol. 12.

Lengel, Edward G., ed., *The Papers of George Washington, Revolutionary War Series, December 1777–February 1778.* Vol. 13. Charlottesville: University of Virginia Press, 2003.

———. *The Papers of George Washington, Revolutionary War Series, May–June 1778.* Vol. 15. Charlottesville: University of Virginia Press, Rotunda, 2003. Vol. 15.

Hoth, David R., ed. *The Papers of George Washington, Revolutionary War Series, July–September 1778.* Vol. 16. Charlottesville: University of Virginia Press, 2006.

THE WRITINGS OF GEORGE WASHINGTON (37 VOLUMES)

Fitzpatrick, John C., ed. "DATE." *The Writings of George Washington.* Vol. 2. Washington DC: U.S. Government Printing Office, 1931.

———. "TO: DATE." *The Writings of George Washington.* Vol. 3. Washington DC: U.S. Government Printing Office, 1931.

———. "To Lee: Dec. 10, 1776." *The Writings of George Washington.* Vol. 6. Washington DC: U.S. Government Printing Office, 1932.

———. "DATE OF LETTER." *The Writings of George Washington.* Vol. 17. Washington DC: U.S. Government Printing Office, 1937.

———. "To Rochambeau, September 8, 1780." *The Writings of George Washington.* Vol. 20. Washington DC: U.S. Government Printing Office, 1937.

———. "DATE/TITLE." *The Writings of George Washington.* Vol. 21. Washington DC: U.S. Government Printing Office, 1937.

———. "DATE/TITLE." *The Writings of George Washington.* Vol. 23. Washington DC: U.S. Government Printing Office, 1937.

———. "DATE/TITLE." *The Writings of George Washington.* Vol. 26. Washington DC: U.S. Government Printing Office, 1938.

———. "December 23, 1788." *The Writings of George Washington.* Vol. ??. Washington, DC: U.S. Government Printing Office, 1931–44.

THE PAPERS OF GENERAL NATHANAEL GREENE (13 VOLUMES)

Showman, Richard K., Margaret Cobb, and Robert E. McCarthy, eds. *The Papers of General Nathanael Greene: Vol. 1, December 1766 to December 1776.* Chapel Hill: North Carolina Press, 1976.

———. *The Papers of General Nathanael Greene, Vol. 2: January 1777 to 16 October 1778.* Chapel Hill: North Carolina Press, 1980.

THE PAPERS OF GENERAL NATHANAEL GREENE:

Showman, Richard K., Margaret Cobb, and Robert E. McCarthy, eds. *The Papers of General Nathanael Greene: Vol. 1, December 1766 to December 1776.* Chapel Hill: North Carolina Press, 1976.

Showman, Richard K., Robert E. McCarthy, and Margaret Cobb, eds. *The Papers of General Nathanael Greene: Vol. 2, January 1777 to October 1778.* Chapel Hill: North Carolina Press, 1980.

Showman, Richard K., Robert E. McCarthy, and Elizabeth C. Stevens, eds. *The Papers of General Nathanael Greene: Vol. 3, 18 October 1778 to 10 May 1779.* Chapel Hill: North Carolina Press, 1984.

Showman, Richard K., Elizabeth C. Stevens, and Dennis M. Conrad, eds. *The Papers of General Nathanael Greene: Vol. 4, 11 May 1779 to 31 October 1779.* Chapel Hill: North Carolina Press, 1986.

Carp, Wayne, Richard K. Showman, and Robert E. McCarthy, eds. *The Papers of General Nathanael Greene: Vol. 5, 1 November 1779 to 31 May 1780.* Chapel Hill: North Carolina Press, 1989.

Stevens, Elizabeth C., Richard K. Showman, and Dennis M. Conrad, eds. *The Papers of General Nathanael Greene: Vol. 6, 1 June 1780 to 25 December 1780.* Chapel Hill: North Carolina Press, 1991.

Conrad, Dennis M., ed. *The Papers of General Nathanael Greene: Vol. 7, 26 December 1780 to 29 March 1781.* Chapel Hill: North Carolina Press, 1994.

Conrad, Dennis M., Roger N. Parks, Martha J. King, and Richard K. Showman, eds. *The Papers of General Nathanael Greene: Vol. 8, 30 March 1781 to 10 July 1781.* Chapel Hill: North Carolina Press, 1995.

Parks, Roger N., ed. *The Papers of General Nathanael Greene: Vol. 9, 11 July 1781 to 2 December 1781.* Chapel Hill: North Carolina Press, 1997.

———. *The Papers of General Nathanael Greene: Vol. 10, 3 December 1781 to 6 April 1782.* Chapel Hill: North Carolina Press, 1998.

Parks, Roger N., Elizabeth Stevens, and Nathaniel Shipton, eds. *The Papers of General Nathanael Greene: Vol. 11, 7 April 1782 to 30 September 1782.* Chapel Hill: North Carolina Press, 2000.

Conrad, Dennis M., and Roger N. Parks, eds. *The Papers of General Nathanael Greene: Vol. 12, 1 October 1782 to 21 May 1783.* Chapel Hill: North Carolina Press, 2001.

Parks, Roger N., ed. *The Papers of General Nathanael Greene: Vol. 13, 22 May 1783 to 13 June 1786.* Chapel Hill: North Carolina Press, 2005.

FREEMAN

Young Washington. Vols. 1 and 2 of *George Washington: A Biography.* 1948.

Planter and Patriot. Vol. 3 of *George Washington: A Biography.* 1951.

Leader of the Revolution. Vol. 4 of *George Washington: A Biography.* 1951.

Victory with the Help of France. Vol. 5 of *George Washington: A Biography.* 1952.

Patriot and President. Vol. 6 of *George Washington: A Biography.* 1954.

First in Peace. Vol. 7 of *George Washington: A Biography.* 1957. Carroll, John Alexander, and Mary Wells Ashworth. Based on Freeman's research.

Acknowledgments

I BELIEVE ANY work is a collaboration of efforts. We all owe our successes to those who believed in us, gave us the chance, and supported us with their words and deeds.

I am very grateful to my editor, Stephen Mansfield, for providing me with the opportunity to work on this project. He took a chance and I hope not to disappoint. Thanks also to my copyeditor, Jamie Chavez, who had many wonderful and meaningful suggestions and corrections. She obviously spent many hours correcting the manuscript.

I would also like to thank the staff at the Oral Roberts University Library who assisted me on many occasions with both research and book acquisition. They are wonderful to work with. My colleagues in the History, Humanities, and Government Department were very helpful in covering classes and putting up with my absenteeism. Thanks to the chair, Dr. Michael Hirlinger, who actually recommended me for this project.

Certainly my undergraduate student researchers, Ben Steiger

and Elisabeth Knier deserve a big thank you. Jonathan Hall, the chief undergrad editor/researcher, was invaluable in this project. All of them should go to graduate school and become writers.

Finally, and most importantly, I appreciate the love and support of my family. My wife and children encouraged me when I was down and put up with my many moods. It's hard to believe they still love me.

About the Author

P AUL S . V ICKERY is a professor of history at Oral Roberts University. He has been involved with education for nearly forty years. A counterintelligence officer with the US Army in Germany for three years, Vickery often has study trips with students in Europe and Latin America. He and his wife love cruising and he is also a destination lecturer aboard ships. Vickery has been an Ordained United Methodist pastor for over twenty years and currently pastors two rural Oklahoma churches in Haskell and Porter. He and his wife have four grown children, six grandchildren, and live in Tulsa, Oklahoma.